D1447371

Real Dads Stand Up!

Blue Peacock Press

Real Dads Stand Up!
What Every Single Father Should Know About Child Support,
Rights and Custody
by Alicia M. Crowe

Published by:
Blue Peacock Press
Post Office Box 1011
Nyack, NY 10960
Orders@BluePeacockpress.com
http://www.Realdadsstandup.com

Cover Design by:
Michael Miquez

Disclaimer:

This book is designed to provide general information about custody and child support. However, since individual cases do vary, neither the publisher nor the author can render legal or other professional services to the reader. Readers should consult with a competent professional on specific questions. No attorney-client relationship is created by the purchase or use of this book. The opinions expressed are solely those of the author.

While the author and publisher have thoroughly researched all sources to ensure the accuracy and completeness of the information presented in this book, we assume no responsibilities for errors, inaccuracies, omissions or any other factor that may appear inconsistent.

Important caution to the reader: Laws in various areas are subject to change. This book does not take the place of an attorney's advice based on the latest developments in family law.

ISBN: 0-9764772-0-3

First Edition.

LCCN: 2005922448

This book is for fathers and those who love them.

To my father, Charles Edwin Crowe (1922-2001), just for being there. Rest in peace.

"For we wrestle not against flesh and blood but against powers and principalities, against the rulers of the darkness of this world, against spiritual wickedness in high places."

Ephesians 6:12

Foreword

As a boy growing up during the 60s and 70s, I vividly remember the television shows of the day: "The Courtship of Eddie's Father" "Happy Days," "Sanford and Son," "All In The Family." There were black and white reruns from 50s: Father Knows Best," "Bachelor Father," "The Danny Thomas Show." Fathers were central to the story lines of these shows, reflecting a society that attempted to value motherhood, fatherhood, marriage and family. Zoom to the 21st century, and things have mightily changed. Recently, one could have scanned through the hundreds of channels available to find large numbers of programs where the father was missing: "Jesse," "Judging Amy," "The Parkers." Or in the case of "Desperate Housewives," husbands and fathers are mere physical impediments to the reigned in carnal desires of their "committed" female mates. These shows are probably as reflective of the socio-cultural attitudes of contemporary society in the way that the tube was reflective back in the day. Except now, the father is missing... When did the change happen? When did we "throw the father out with the bathwater"?

David Blankenhorn, in his groundbreaking book "Fatherless America," observed the following: "The United States is becoming an increasingly fatherless society. A generation ago, an American child could reasonably expect to grow up with his or her father. Today, an American child can reasonably expect not to. Fatherlessness is now the most harmful demographic trend of this generation. It is the leading cause of declining child well-being in our society. It is also the engine driving our most urgent social problems, from crime to adolescent pregnancy to child sexual abuse to domestic violence against women. Yet, despite its scale and social consequences, fatherlessness is a problem that is frequently ignored or denied...." Out of the context of a fatherless society,' it becomes pretty clear that the hurdles that many men face in asserting their parental rights are higher than ever. Flowing out of the mother-preferred "tender years" doctrine of family law, to the gender inequity of welfare policy and paternity laws, those hurdles tend to dissuade even the most determined father from battling with "the system" in order to perform meaningful parenting to their children.

Since the 1960s, our society has suffered from "multiple personality disorder" with respect to its attitudes about men and parenting. We want husbands to be providers and nurturers, yet, we don't want marriage to be too confining. We want divorced dads to step up and finance their children's lives, but, we don't want to enforce their custody and visitation rights. We tell single, about-to-be fathers that legally, life does not begin at conception, only to turn around and say to them after a child is born out-of-wedlock, "you'd better pay for the child that you conceived." Should a father have to fight the various negative forces aligned against his parenting? No. Though, he shouldn't have to fight, yet, he must. Why must he fight? For, the specter of manless, fatherless communities is already being manifested in some sectors of the nation. In them, young males look to street gangs for older male guidance, rather than their fathers and grandfathers, who've been marginalized out of their lives. Young women, suffering from "father hunger," expose themselves to predatory relationships from the same young men seeking their own way. Recovery, for many of these neighborhoods, where the descendants of the Middle Passage, slavery, and Jim Crow once blossomed, now seems distant (if possible, at all…).

Recently, some social commentators have begun to inveigh a call for men to "man up." Some years ago, a group referring to itself as the "Promise Keepers," corralled thousands of men into football stadiums, asking them to be dedicated husbands and fathers. A decade ago, approximately one million African American men gathered in the nation's capitol, engaging in "Promise Keeper"-like pledges. Yet, none of these movements offered any specific information as to how men navigate the various political/legal land mines that undermine their parenting. Attorney Alicia Crowe, within the pages of this book, gives fathers a much-needed resource: a primer on how to interact with the family law system. She simplifies the legal process, cutting through the confusing legal jargon, making it easy for the layperson to understand and maneuver the custody and child support system. This book helps dads do what they absolutely need to do to understand the laws and process. Alicia takes you step by step through the legal process as though she were right there with you. You will be better able to find and work with legal representation. She gives away valuable legal information that would ordinarily cost thousands of dollars. Every chapter in this book will help fathers gain the strength and confidence needed to win. Alicia motivates and energizes fathers to be better parents. Having seen her in action both in the courtroom and in family seminars, I can, without reservation, say that she may be the foremost legal mind regarding fathers and the legal system within our borders. She's tough, yet a background in civil rights activism (through her family and through legal training), has given her a unique perspective on the practice of family law, and how fathers can traverse its anti-father bias.

BILL STEPHNEY
stepsunmusic@msn.com

Acknowledgments

I would like to acknowledge the following people who have made this effort possible. Thank you to my mother, Gwendolyn Crowe, and my father, the late Charles Edwin Crowe, who encouraged me to stand up for fathers and everything else that I believe in. Daddy, thank you for showing me how to stand up by setting the example and picketing the Ku Klux Klan in Stone Mountain, Georgia.

Thank you to my sister and law partner Alice T. Crowe-Bell, for standing by me every step of this journey. Thanks to the late Alice Crowe Garner, (Auntie), a prolific writer. Thanks to the Crowe family for being my rock, and the Stinson family, for reminding me why fathers matter.

Special thanks to my editor and teacher, Louis Reyes Rivera, and to my brother-in-law, Curtis Bell, for his technical genius in recovering my manuscript when I lost it on my computer twice, my mentor, the late Conrad Lynn, Esq., Dr. Lez Edmond and William Stephney, for your consistency in doing all of the things that make your commitment to this movement genuine.

Thanks to Malik Yoba for broadening my vision on alternatives to court, Camille Yarbrough, for telling me to "Do what the spirit says do," Rev. Conrad Tillard, Robert Cash, Yvonne Alston, Jenny Botts, Judith Albury, Efrain Rodriguez, Eric Legette, Thabiti Boone, Stacey Brooks Scott, Shantal Auguste, Amber Kirkwood, Michelle Reed Bowman, Esq., Leslie Jones Thomas, Esq., Catherine Miklitsch, Esq., Dennis Adjei-Brenyah, Esq., Polly Chill, Esq. Peter Holoman, Dr. Edison Jackson, Patricia M. Worthy, Esq., Dr. Stanley L. Ralph, Hon. Percy Sutton, Peter G. Holden, Leon Taylor, the late Albert Holland, Esq., Marie Brown, Medgar Evers College, Iowan Tribal (Yolanda), Viola Plummer, Amadi Ajamu, Loren Mulraine, Esq., Tusca Alexis, Esq., Mary Lynn Nicolas-Brewster, Esq., Allura Scott, Esq., Terry Morris, Esq., Lee Clayton Goodman, Esq., Bruce Jackson, Esq., Julius Crowe Hampton, Rajeen Persuad, Ed Kirkland, Chiz Schultz, Juanita Burnett C.P.A., Dr. A.J. Everet Green, Min. Kevin Muhammad, and to my fellow members of the Louis Reyes Rivera Writers Workshop at Sistas' Place.

CONTENTS

About the Author

Alicia M. Crowe is a family court practitioner in New York who has represented fathers and mothers in family court cases for nearly a decade. She is a partner in the law firm of Crowe & Crowe. In addition, Alicia is a writer, performer and lecturer. She has developed a series of unique workshops based on her experiences litigating family court issues. She has a degree in Political Science from Adelphi University and a Law degree from Howard University School of Law, and is a member to the New York and Connecticut Bars.

To contact Alicia Crowe, please write or e-mail her at this Address:

Blue Peacock Press
P.O. Box 1011
Nyack, New York 10960
(845) 348-1160

www.Bluepeacockpress.com

e-mail: Alicia@thefatherfriendlyguide.com

Introduction

You may have already discovered, as I did, that the custody and child support system in family court is not very father friendly. Mothers are often walked through the process, while fathers are expected to navigate alone. If you have ever been down this road, please know that I share your frustration. However, through my years of practicing law, I have also discovered that there are two other very significant reasons fathers do not fare well in custody and child support proceedings.

First, fathers do not really know how the system works. Unlike fathers, mothers take time to learn the system. They ask questions and seek out information. Mothers follow up on the results.

Second, many fathers lack the necessary organizational skills to help them maneuver a difficult and challenging custody and child support enforcement system. Consequently, fathers find themselves caught in the grip of the child support trap and losing access to their children.

So, I wrote this book especially for fathers like you who are stepping up to the plate and trying to do the right thing. This book is based on material I present at colleges and conferences throughout the country and my experiences as a lawyer. For over a decade, the information has helped many of my clients. It can help you too. Ask yourself the following questions:

Has your Ex just served you with a summons and petition for child support and you want to know how much you will have to pay?

Do you already have a child support order? If so, are your child support payments taken out of your paycheck?

Has your driver's license been suspended?

Is your Ex receiving public assistance?

Have you been ordered to appear in court for child support violation?

Is your Ex refusing to let you see your children?

Do you want legal custody of your child?

If you have answered yes to any of these questions, then you are in good company. Real Dads Stand Up is the book for you. There are a number of great books available on the topic of custody and child support, but for the most part they have two major weaknesses: the material is often written from the mother's point of view and makes very little reference to fathers; the material is written in such a way that it is difficult to follow.

Based on my experience as a lawyer representing fathers in family court for over a decade, I am able to present this information in a way that readers can understand. The concepts in this book are presented in a question-and-answer format. To make it easy to follow, I highlight key points in boldface and offer you a simple step-by-step tool that teaches you how to navigate the often challenging and lengthy custody and child support system.

Every year thousands of fathers just like you go into custody and/or child support proceedings in family court. When they know what to do, they can get through it successfully. Now, you can too. You can maneuver the system. Yes, it is possible. You can avoid the child support trap and maintain access to your children.

This straightforward easy-to-read book tells you how the child support system works. First, it explains the courtroom process. Second, it defines paternity and child support and how it is established. Third, it shows you how to get organized, and how and where to find an attorney. It explains the courtroom process.

Next, it helps to outline what is likely to happen in court. After court, we discuss how to follow up on your child support order, and what to do if your situation changes and you can't pay child support. We then discuss the child support enforcement process and what can happen to you if you do not pay your child support as ordered. As you read through this book, you will find valuable information and tools to help you deal with the child support enforcement agency.

Then we move into custody and what judges consider when deciding custody and/or visitation. In addition, this book explains what you can do when your Ex won't let you see your children.

We then outline alternatives to litigation like settlement and mediation.

Finally, this book provides answers to the most commonly asked questions on custody and child support and offers key resources to help you and other fathers exercise your rights. My father called it "the stick to beat back with."

Careful! This book is not intended to be a substitute for legal advice. Many of the examples and references are based on New York law. The laws in your state may differ. Consult a competent family lawyer for your particular case.

1

Deadbeat Dad or Just Dead Broke

We have often heard about the "Deadbeat Dad." You know, that abominable creature who, when ordered to pay child support, thumbs his nose up at the system. All fathers who don't pay child support are not deadbeat dads. Deadbeats are defined as those fathers who can afford to pay child support but choose not to. Accordingly, these dads also have the time and means to dedicate to their children but choose not to.

Deadbeats are the types of fathers who put their interests above the interests of their children. They are self-absorbed, physically or emotionally unavailable, walking around looking and smelling good, sporting new clothes and fancy shoes. They will live and sleep in a house with another woman and her children, but they won't take care of their own. Instead of paying child support, they buy expensive toys like sports cars, motorcycles, carry cell phones and the latest electronic gadgets, and make excuses for not providing for their children's basic needs. When they finally get caught and are legally forced to accept their parental responsibility, they are the main ones who cry, "The system is not fair." If this sounds like you, then hold on.

Dead Broke

There are also the dads who are there for their children. They love and want to nurture their children, and their children love them. However, many of these dads, often young and poor, have little or no education or skills to find and maintain employment. In other words, they are dead broke and have no ability to pay child support or earn enough to sustain their families. Many of these fathers may have been raised in homes without their own fathers and struggle to figure out how to be men by accepting full responsibility. This group also includes the working guy who pays what he can when he can. Unfortunately, these are the ones who end up paying for the sins of the deadbeats. Dead broke dads who don't know they have rights end up going to jail for not paying child support.

Beating the Deadbeats

Surely, you may be among those who do pay child support, but that is not all there is to being a father. Fathers are more than just checks in the mail. Fathers matter.

Real Dads are fathers who also provide the emotional and psychological support that goes with parenthood. That means loving, nurturing, caring and being there for your child despite the failed relationship with the other parent.

Don't get trapped into believing that the only thing that you have to give your child is money. Think about your own relationship with your father. How did it feel to have or not have your father play an active role in your life?

To be successful, you must learn how to deal with the family court and child support system. First, you must accept the fact that the child support laws and enforcement program are not fair. The process is not there to help you and is not exactly "father friendly." For that reason, you must help yourself. In order to win, you must play the game. Real dads don't win by dodging and fleeing their financial responsibility and turning into a real "deadbeat dad." To play and win, you must know the rules.

Now, let the games begin.

Notes:

Notes:

2

What Do You Want, Really?

To establish paternity?
To pay, establish or modify child support?
To have visitation rights (enforced)?
To gain full custody?

Choices fathers have to make

Understand that when you go to court, there is only one issue (or one specific matter) before the court and which the judge has to weigh. If child support is the central issue, then the issues of visitation and custody will, generally speaking, not be heard. If visitation is the issue, then nothing else will be heard. Whichever parent initiates the proceedings often determines which issue is going to be heard before the judge. You must decide on which issue you wish to bring before the court: (a) Custody; (b) Visitation; (c) Child Support, etc.

How do you approach your situation?

How you approach your situation can make a big difference in the outcome of your case in family court. If you are like most fathers, the thought of stepping into court is absolutely terrifying. Going through the legal process can trigger all kinds of negative feelings like anger, confusion, fear, insecurity and doubt. The moment you get served with court papers, whether you react, respond or initiate your case can mean the difference between being able to spend quality-parenting time with your children and going to jail for not paying child support. Recently, in Kentucky, a judge gave a father who did not pay child support the option of going to jail or getting a vasectomy.

Do you…react?

"If you always do what you always did, you always get what you always got."

--Moms Mabley

According to poet Louis Reyes Rivera, we always have three options: we can react; we can respond; we can initiate. If all we do is react to our situation, we may think we are in control, but we are really not. Our vision is clouded and we are trapped by our emotions. Instead of planning and taking the necessary steps to deal with the situation, we get angry and lose it. When we react without first thinking about the situation, we usually end up regretting what we have done and wishing we could turn back the hands of time.

Just when we are about to be penalized, we ask ourselves, "How did I get here?"

What we don't realize is that when all we do is react, our responses become so predictable that we play right into the hands of others, especially our adversaries. It's as if their hands are holding a remote control and all they have to do is push the right buttons, and we go right into reaction mode.

Our adversaries already know what we will likely do even before we do it. Judges and the people involved in the legal system know this too because they deal with many cases, and they see reactionary types every day. Some expect us to just get angry and do nothing more; some even get happy when we don't assert our rights because it makes their jobs a lot easier.

When all we do is react, we never get the results that we truly desire. Our concerns never get addressed. Because we don't take any action on our behalf, we cut off our options and lose out on opportunities to be heard. When confronted with challenges or obstacles, we cave in too quickly. When we are being sued for paternity and child support, we don't file for custody or parenting time with our children—or, after sitting in distress in the family court waiting room for twenty minutes, we will agree to anything just to get out of there. I have witnessed too many fathers who, out of frustration and haste, quickly scribble their name on the bottom of settlement agreements that essentially gave away their rights.

Some of us can become so paralyzed by the thought of dealing with the legal system that we freeze up and do nothing at all. We don't show up to court. We don't consult with a lawyer. We don't pursue our rights, or even find out what rights we have. We take no responsibility at all. Instead, we do nothing but let the legal hammer fall where it may, and it usually does, right on our heads.

Let me tell you about Tony. He was so angry when his Ex served him with child support violation papers that he took it as a criticism and personal attack on his fatherhood. He could not believe it. "How could she do this to me? I take care of my children! Why is she dragging me into the system like that? If she thinks I'm going to pay her one '$%%#' dime, she's got another thing coming. I'll just go to jail," he cried.

Tony did not consult with a lawyer to find out what his rights were. He did not try to resolve the issue with his Ex, nor did he respond to the court papers. He didn't initiate any proceeding of his own to secure access to his children.

Instead, he just showed up to court wearing his emotions on his sleeve, hoping to just tell the judge his side of the story, and somehow the judge would see things his way and rule in his favor.

Not so! Instead, the judge threw him in jail for failing to pay child support. Now he not only lost his freedom, but he can't see his children, and he still owes child support.

The truth of the matter is that Tony was really scared to go into court. He put up a front, the macho routine; he felt the court was out to send him to jail anyway, so he took the easy way out. That's what he came to expect from the legal system. He didn't have a lot of money. He did not have a father growing up, so he felt cheated. He even believed he was trying to be there for his children the best way he knew how.

When his Ex served him with child support papers, he got angry. He could not understand why she would drag him into court. Tony did not trust the legal system. He felt like someone was trying to put a dollar amount on his fatherhood. Because communication had already broken down between him and his children's mother, they ended up on opposite sides of the courtroom in Family Court.

What Tony didn't realize is that when one person, in this case, the mother, is taking more of the responsibility for raising and providing for the children's basic needs than the other parent, that parent gets angry too. She feels hurt and snubbed. If the father has either not responded or simply reacted negatively toward her attempts at getting the help and support she needs, she may feel that court is her last and only resort.

11

Do you ...respond?

When we respond, instead of letting our emotions get the best of us, our intellect takes charge. We are actually thinking about the situation before we do anything. Instead of going into our usual mode of reacting, we stop and think. We ask questions like...What do I really want to happen? How do I go about getting that result? By changing the way we see the problem, we open up to new information, and with that information, we can plan our strategy and move ahead.

When we allow ourselves the chance to think, our minds transcend limitation. We find out what we need to know in order to deal with the situation; we realize that information is power. Armed with new information we are able to properly defend ourselves. For example, it's the first court appearance on your custody or child support case. The judge arraigns you (informs you of the charges and asks if you plead guilty or not guilty) and advises you as to your rights to an attorney. Now you have an opportunity to stop and evaluate your situation. Here is where most fathers get spooked and panic about going to court.

Did you know that if you show up to court and tell the judge that you would like time to get an attorney, the judge would usually grant you a reasonable adjournment for a week or two to enable you to seek representation? Many fathers don't know this, and they get so stressed out about going to court that they don't show up. When you know the process, you can be ready. You don't have to panic.

By asking the court for a reasonable adjournment (extension of time) to seek legal representation, you give yourself the chance to consult with an attorney to explore your options (or at least to take advantage of the free consultation). You get to step away from the canvas, take a good look at your situation and ask for necessary help. It may be just enough time to finish reading this book and planning your strategy.

To be responsive means to get a lawyer, go to the library, get a book on the subject, get your paperwork in order, show up to court, and file response papers. While this is the intelligent way to go, respondents are limited. When all we do is respond, we do only what the situation calls for and nothing more. We don't create possibilities. Instead, we limit our options to just what is on the table. Consequently, the court can't grant us anything more than what is before it.

For example, if you only respond to petition for child support, instead of filing for custody or visitation rights/parenting time, then the result may be that you still won't get to see your children. Don't forget. The judge can rule only on the matter that was brought to the court's attention.

Do you ...initiate?

When we initiate, we not only study the possibilities, we envision how and why we want what we do. We define the action we're going to take. People who initiate know that no matter how hard they plan their work, it won't work unless they do. When we initiate, we don't wait for something to happen; we make the first move. We see the big picture, and we create alternatives.

Too many fathers make the huge mistake of walking into court thinking that all they have to do is tell the judge their side of the story and somehow, like the wiz, the judge will rule in their favor. When served with child support papers, instead of just paying child support and calling it a day, initiators file for visitation rights/parenting time or go for custody. We get involved in a fatherhood support group. We become active and proactive. We take risks. We stand up. We are not put off by what other people do because we are determined to not let anything or anyone get the best of us.

What do you want to happen? How are you going to go about getting that result? Remember, when we initiate, we are in control of our emotions. We use our intellect to respond and defend ourselves, but we don't limit ourselves to being reactionary or becoming intellectual robots. When we initiate, we empower ourselves. We seek out the people and information to help us. We see obstacles as opportunities. We stay focused on the positive. We do more than just respond to the situation. We don't waste time criticizing the other parent or trying to control her through our behavior. We are able to put our negative feelings aside for the good of our children. We realize that it's not about her; it's not about winning. It's about the children. We keep the faith and we keep moving ahead.

"Don't forget that we are emotional and intellectual and imaginative," poet Louis Reyes Rivera reminds us. "The question is not which of the three we will do (react, respond, initiate), but which of the three will guide the other two!"

Notes:

Notes:

Notes:

3

How Child Support Proceedings Begin

"Will I see my children again, and how much will I have to pay?"

The relationship is over. It's time to move on. In New York, if you and the other parent were never married, the proceeding will take place generally in Family Court.

However, if you and the other parent are married, then a divorce or separation action may be begun. These types of cases are not heard in Family Court; the family court does not have jurisdiction (authority) to grant a divorce; however, it does have concurrent jurisdiction with State Supreme Court to hear issues relating to custody, child support, spousal support, visitation and family offenses. These types of proceedings may still be filed in Family Court. This enables the parties to resolve these issues ahead of time in Family Court, making it easier to obtain a divorce in Supreme Court.

She just served you with papers

Child support proceedings begin when your child's mother files a family court petition against you, asking a judge to order child support. Then she has you served with the court papers. Fathers who have custody may also file a petition for child support against the other parent.

The summons

The first paper is usually a Summons. It is usually served along with a complaint/petition. A summons is an order from the court notifying a person that he or she is being sued. The summons tells you when and where you have to go to court. It also gives you a certain amount of days to respond to the complaint, either by filing a written answer or risk losing your case by default. For example, in New York, you have twenty days to respond to a summons.

Each state has its own official form of summons and requirements for filling it out. To make it easier, I included a sample summons in the Appendix B. You can also go to the court clerk's office to get a copy of one.

The petition

The next paper you will receive will usually be the Petition. A petition tells you the legal claims made against you and what you are to do to respond to the lawsuit. On the petition, the title of the case usually reads, "The County of ...(home county) on behalf of minor child against John Doe." In New York, the petition may not state the county; it may just list the petitioner. It may only list the county or Commissioner of Social Services if they are the ones filing the petition.

When the petition is filed in Family Court, the court clerk assigns a docket number to the case. This is how the court identifies the case. This number will appear on all documents filed in the case as well as on the child support order.

Figure 1.

In the County of Dullsville
On behalf of Minor Child

Jane Smith,   Petition for Child Support
                 Petitioner,   Docket No.: P-000-01
                 vs.

Joe Doe

                 Respondent

Usually the petition or summons and complaint will be served (delivered) on you. In New York, service in Family Court can take place by mail in lieu of personal service. If a summons and complaint are served on you, you must respond by filing an Answer with the clerk of the court. Your response must be filed within the short time frame allowed by law.

If your child was born out of wedlock, and the child resides with the other parent, the child support petition may be a combined support/paternity petition.

A paternity suit is one matter before the court. A corresponding child support case is often viewed as a separate matter. Once paternity has been established, a child support order may be set. The process of setting child support varies from state to state. Sometimes, when paternity (legal fatherhood) is established after a contested action, the Hearing Examiner or Support Magistrate will also set an amount of child support as part of the paternity case. In some states, courts hold a separate proceeding to set the amount of child support. Chances are, if you established paternity by signing the voluntary acknowledgement form, there will usually be a separate case and hearing to determine the amount of child support to be paid. Otherwise, if the parties are not married, and there has been no prior determination or Acknowledgment of Paternity, then paternity must be established as a matter of law.

Read the summons carefully. It usually contains provisions that must be followed. For example, you may be required to provide proof of your income and assets. You may also be notified that an order of support will be made on the return date of the summons and that your failure to appear in court may result in suspension of your driver's license, business license, or recreational license or permits.

A Word of Caution

If you receive any notice stating that you must appear in court, do not ignore it. You may feel like crawling under a rug and hiding. That is the worst thing you could do. Be proactive. Protect your rights. **Read all papers carefully. If there is something you don't understand, contact a lawyer immediately.** Don't wait until the last minute. Remember, there are two sides to every story; make sure you get to tell yours. **If you do not properly respond to divorce, paternity, child support, or custody papers in a timely fashion, you may not be allowed to object later.** All states have statutes of limitations that govern the period of time in which a lawsuit may be filed. Check to see whether the petition is timely. By ignoring court papers you could be waiving valuable rights.

Avoid Default

After you are served, you must respond to court papers within the short time frame allowed by law. If you are served with a petition, make note of the date the petition was filed. The date and time will usually be stamped on the front page of the petition. This is important **because you could be liable for child support from the date the petition was actually filed.** This is known as retroactive child support. This is also how arrears (back child support payments) are established. So if the court date

19

gets adjourned (postponed), your final order of child support may tell you that you have to pay from the date the petition was filed and not when that final child support order is made.

DEFAULT- A default judgment legally establishes a child support order and opens the way for the collection process to begin.

What happens if I don't show up in court?
"The first time I learned about my court date was when my wages were garnished," he said. This may sound like a good reason, but it's not an excuse.

You cannot afford to take the issue of paternity lightly. Nor can you afford to ignore court papers with which you have been served. If you don't appear in court to contest paternity in the initial stages, the consequences can be devastating. Some fathers do not learn they owe child support until their arrears (unpaid child support payments) have grown to thousands of dollars, and the money is taken out of their paychecks every week. This may occur because you did not appear in court at the date and time the court expected you to appear.

The court may issue an arrest warrant forcing you to be brought before the court. This is more common in child support enforcement proceedings.

In some states, your failure to answer a summons or notice to appear in court will inevitably lead to a child support order by default. Courts enter a default order against a respondent who does not appear in court or who does not properly answer the complaint, either by filing a written answer with the court responding to the complaint, or by entering into a voluntary stipulation for child support. Some courts may make a temporary child support order based on the needs of the child and adjourn the case to give the respondent a chance to appear.

Scenario: Joe gets served with paternity papers. He is furious and telephones the Child Support Enforcement Agency (CSEA) and the court. Joe says, "I don't know what you're talking about. I am not the father. This is ridiculous. I am not going to court."

Joe does not show up to court, thinking that the case will go away. Not so. What Joe just did was give the court and the CSEA the green light to get a default judgment against him and collect child support.

A Note on Due Process

Due process requires you to be given notice and opportunity to be heard. There are rules as to how legal papers are properly served.

One of the first things that should be addressed in court is whether you were properly served. If you are served with papers, make a habit of checking the postmarks and certificate of service against the actual date you received the notice. Also make a note of how you received the papers and who delivered them to you. You need to know whether you were actually served with the summons and petition and if so, whether the method of service was proper under the law.

If the method of service was not proper, then your attorney usually objects on the record to the manner of service on the first court appearance. If the petitioner is not able to show the court that you were served properly, by showing the court an affidavit or statement of service, then the Support Magistrate may dismiss the case.

However, in order to prevail, you must show up to court and raise the objection. If you show up to court and do not object to the manner in which service of process was made, there is a presumption that you were properly served.

What if I can't make the court appearance?

If you are not able to make the court date for whatever reason, you must put it in writing before the scheduled court date. It is up to the Support Magistrate or hearing officer to grant you a continuance. If the court grants you a continuance, you will be given a new date to appear. It's a good idea to follow up with a telephone call to see if your request has been granted. Remember, until the Court tells you otherwise, you must appear for your scheduled court date.

You can appear by telephone

Under the Uniform Interstate Family Support Act (UIFSA), you may be allowed to waive your physical appearance and testify by telephone or other electronic means to avoid default. In order to do this, however, you have to complete an electronic testimony application and file a waiver of personal appearance before your court date. Find out if you can qualify in your area. For example, some states, like New York, have permission forms on the Internet (See www.courts.state.ny.us).

Notes:

Notes:

4

Going to Court

You are not alone in Family Court

As the divorce rate and out-of-wedlock birthrate rises, for many, the family court is becoming a fact of life. More people are likely to encounter the family court system than any other type of court proceeding. Family Court was originally created to take action on behalf of children, spouses and parents. It has a broad scope of powers to address the particular needs of the people who come before it.

For instance, Family Court has the power to hear cases involving paternity, child support, custody, visitation, family offenses, child neglect, and termination of parental rights. It also has jurisdiction over matters involving adoption, guardianship, juvenile delinquency, and persons in need of supervision. More than likely, the first time you come into contact with the family court system is through a child support proceeding.

Unlike other courts, there are no juries in Family Court; the judge or Support Magistrate decides your case. Family Court is generally open to the public; however, the judge hearing a case may decide to close the courtroom or exclude certain persons, based on the privacy interests of the parties, and/or possible harm to the children. Due to the private nature of the matters involved, cameras are not allowed in the courtroom. The file records in Family Court are strictly confidential and are not open to the general public. If you are directly involved in a case, you are among the few who can get copies of most documents in the court's case file. It is a good idea to go to court before your scheduled court date to review your file, if you want to. When you go to court, make sure you bring your driver's license or some other photo identification with you.

Who's who in the Court?

There are a number of people involved in a child support or custody/visitation case in Family Court.

The Court Officer(s) are equivalent to street police, though only in the courthouse. They carry guns.

The Court Clerk usually sits next to the judge. This person assists the judge in keeping the files and court calendar in order. Get to know court clerks; they have a wealth of information that may assist you in your case.

The Court Stenographer is the one who types everything that is said in court. Sometimes the cases are recorded on audiotape. In support proceedings and in other types of Family Court proceedings in New York, electronic recording devices are used instead of stenographers.

Parties refer to you and the other parent. The person who filed the case is called the moving party or the petitioner. The person who the case is filed against is the responding party or the respondent. If you are representing yourself, you are pro se. If you have an attorney, then as Counsel that person represents you.

Child Support Collection Unit (CSCU) and/or **Child Support Enforcement Agency (CSEA)** is the agency that collects and enforces child support orders by filing violations on behalf of persons entitled to receive support payments. Although the CSCU, has links to Family Court, it is a separate agency.

The Support Magistrate, also known as the referee or the hearing officer, is the fact-finder in paternity and child support cases. He or she supervises the courtroom and makes the decision that becomes your child support order. The support magistrate's decision can be appealed to a Family Court judge.

The Family Court Judge can make orders regarding paternity, custody, visitation, etc. While the support hearing Magistrate can only determine child support, the Family Court Judge has greater authority. The Judge's Secretary manages the caseload for the judge. The secretary sets hearings and can answer basic questions about the court procedures.

The County Attorney or **Corporation Counsel** is an attorney who represents the state or municipality. This person assumes legal representation over and for the children involved.

Assigned Counsel or **Court Appointed Attorney**. Generally, a judge will appoint a lawyer to represent a person who is charged with committing a crime and who cannot afford an attorney. In some states, a court may appoint an attorney in a paternity action or in a case where the defendant is facing criminal charges for failing to pay child support. In Family Court, Assigned Counsel may be appointed (even though the case is civil) due to contempt or willfulness hearings because of the possibility of a term of jail. Court appointed attorneys are not always free. Some states may hold the client responsible to pay a portion of the legal fees involved in the entire process.

The Petitioner's Attorney is the attorney for the person who started the legal proceedings. Your wife's attorney is the one who represents her. If the father brings the proceedings, he may be the petitioner.

The Respondent's Attorney is a private attorney who represents the person being sued. This will be your attorney. Your need for an attorney more or less depends on how well you understand the legal issues and what steps you have to take. While you are certainly entitled to represent yourself in your child support proceeding, it is wise to retain the services of a family law attorney when you are required to go to court.

Things to remember

When you go to court, first, make sure you know how to get there. Bring your Notice to Appear in Court that states the name of the Support Magistrate or hearing officer and the date and time of your hearing. It is a good idea to write down the time and date and location on your contact sheet. Most courts usually open at 9:00AM. If you are scheduled to appear when the court opens, try to arrive extra early to avoid long lines. When you get to court, be prepared to sit and wait for hours. You may want to bring something to read. Remember to bring your court file with you. In chapter six, I explain how to create one.

Whatever you do, don't bring your new girlfriend or significant other to court. Her presence will only irritate your child's mother and make it impossible to settle the matter peacefully. You also don't want to prejudice the judge.

Once you enter the courthouse, you will have to pass through a security check set up by court officers. You may be searched and asked to remove items from your person. It's not a good idea to wear a lot of jewelry or carry unnecessary items. You may be asked to check them. Don't bring knives or other weapons or sharp objects either. Courts take a lot of precautions to ensure the safety of the people coming into court. In Family Court, tensions run high. It is very likely that people may bring weapons to court in order to hurt someone. Don't be surprised if there are surveillance cameras watching you.

The clerk's office is where you go to file papers, such as petitions, answers and motions, and to pick up a copy of the court rules and child support guidelines. There is usually a file room where you can also review your file.

The waiting room is where you sit and wait for your case to be called. At times, it can get very crowded; so make sure that you sign in with a court officer who lets the judge know you are present. Although you may arrive to court on time, be prepared to sit and wait for hours before your case is actually called. This is a good time to try and resolve the matter with the other party, if possible. The attorneys usually do this. If a settlement agreement cannot be reached, just stay seated and wait for your case to be called. When the judge is ready to see you, a court officer will call your name and escort you in to see the judge.

Personal appearance

When you walk into a courtroom, the judge or decision maker can tell a lot about you just by looking at what you wear. Remember, "First impressions are lasting impressions." You want to make sure that when you go to court, you dress like someone who has respect for himself and his children. In other words, dress like a "father." If this poses a problem for you, then you must decide whether your "look" is more important than your children. When deciding what to wear, keep in mind that flashy designer clothes give the judge or Support Magistrate the impression that you can afford to pay a lot of money. On the other hand, looking grungy and unkempt shows disrespect for the court and yourself. Here are a few tips:

Do:

1. Do keep a well-shaven face and a good haircut.
2. Do wear a well-ironed white or blue collared shirt and a simple necktie.
3. Do wear Khaki, gray or navy pants and leather belt.
4. You can wear a dark colored suit, like navy, brown or gray.
5. Sport jackets work well in navy or gray and are to be worn with matching shirt and pants.
6. Do wear slip-on shoes or laced shoes that are polished.

Don't:

1. Don't dress like you are about to play a pick-up basketball game. Don't wear baseball caps, tee shirts, tank tops, sweatshirts, shorts, or sweat suits.

2. Don't wear your favorite nightclub outfit. Family court is not a party.

3. Don't wear sneakers no matter how expensive.

4. Don't wear flashy gold chains, rings, bracelets or earrings. Besides, you will have trouble passing the metal detector search.

5. By all means, stay away from day-glow or bright candy colored suits.

How you act in court is just as important as how you look. Here are a few tips:

The Waiting Room

1. When you enter the waiting room, don't forget to sign in with the court officers.

2. Don't sit next to your Ex or her attorney.

3. Don't start an argument in the waiting room or feed into one with the other side, no matter how tempting. Court officers are the eyes and ears of the court. They are watching you. Surveillance cameras may be watching you too.

Before you go into the courtroom

1. Remember to turn off your beeper and/or cellular phone.

2. Remove your headphones and hats.

3. Always follow the court officer's direction.

While in the courtroom

1. Rise when the judge enters the courtroom.

2. The judge or Support Magistrate will ask you to state your name and address for the court record. Then, a court officer will ask you to raise your right hand and ask you to either swear or affirm to tell the truth. Be careful. This is the first opportunity for the court to observe your demeanor. What you say and how you say it sets the tone. You want to make a good impression.

3. Address the judge (the court) by "Your Honor" or simply "judge" not Miss or Mister.

4. Don't ever interrupt the judge. Wait until (s)he has spoken, then ask if you may be heard or ask your attorney if you should speak. Remember that everything you say is being recorded.

5. When addressing the judge (the court), present yourself with dignity. Make strong eye contact and speak up so everyone in the court room can hear you. Remember that you are being recorded. Speak clearly so that nothing is lost in the recording or transcription.

6. Child support hearings can be very adversarial. The other side will say things that may touch a nerve. Try to keep your emotions in check. What you say, how you say it sounds different when you are angry. Do not show your anger or dismay with the judge, with any witness, or with the opposing side.

7. Do not interrupt the other parties when they are testifying, no matter how much you disagree with what they are saying. You will have your turn to speak.

8. Listen carefully to the question asked and only answer the question asked. Do not change the subject or ramble on.

9. Tell the truth. Remember that you are under oath.

Show up on time

If you are scheduled to appear in Family Court, you are expected to arrive at the courthouse on time. If you are not there when your case is called, the judge or Support Magistrate may go ahead and decide the case without you, or may dismiss the case, especially if the other party does not show up. If you're there and the petitioner does not show up, the case may be dismissed without prejudice, meaning that the petitioner may bring the case back into court again. In certain cases involving serious charges, when you do not appear in court, the judge may order that a bench warrant be issued for your arrest. Now in all states, a parent can make a request to waive his/her appearance and give testimony over the telephone. Find out how to go about doing this in your state.

The first court appearance

On your first court appearance, the Hearing Examiner or Support Magistrate is required by law to inform you of the contents of the petition and explain your legal rights to you. This stage of the process is known as the arraignment. At this point, you should tell the judge that you want to get an attorney. You have a right to one. The judge will grant you an adjournment (extension of time, usually a week or two) to get an attorney.

This also gives you the chance to plan your strategy or work out a settlement with the other parent. These proceedings can move very quickly.

You don't have to make any statements. You don't have to agree to anything. Too many fathers make the mistake of running their mouths to the court. Remember, anything and everything you say can and will be used against you later. Unless you and the other parent have worked out an agreement, it's best not to say anything without consulting with an attorney.

If during this appearance, you show up to court without an attorney, you must be given a copy of the chart of the basic formula used to calculate child support. Make sure you get a copy.

How do I find a lawyer?

When it comes to finding a lawyer, if you're like most people, you don't know where to begin. For many, the mere thought of interviewing a lawyer can be just as scary as going to court. In fact, the entire experience can be paralyzing. Because lawyers have a reputation for coming across as "figures of authority," we are uncomfortable asking them the questions. The good news is that after reading this chapter, you won't be afraid of lawyers. If anything, you will be in a better position to assess whether you even need a lawyer at all and, of course, how best to access one.

Word of mouth

Word of mouth is the best method for finding a lawyer. Friends or family members can be very helpful in recommending an attorney, especially if they have gone through a similar situation. There is nothing better than a satisfied customer to recommend an attorney. Ask someone you know to recommend an attorney.

Bar Associations/ Legal referral services

You can also contact your local bar association to find a lawyer. Bar associations are organizations for lawyers (i.e., the National Bar Association). Most bar associations have lawyer referral programs that can put you in touch with family lawyers in your area. They don't recommend one lawyer over another. However, this is a good way to make contact with an attorney. After meeting more than one attorney, you can decide which one to hire or not.

Non-profit organizations may offer legal services, or some law schools offer legal clinics that take family law cases at low cost or at no charge. With the legal clinics, you would be assigned a senior law student who is supervised by an attorney/law professor to represent you. Here again, word of mouth is a good way to find a clinic. Satisfied clients make the best referrals.

Yellow pages

Lawyers are really not hard to find. Many lawyers advertise in telephone directories. You can look in the telephone directory under Attorneys or Lawyers. A lot of lawyers place ads detailing their specialties. Some lawyers will even list the specific areas of practice, such as child support, custody, visitation, etc. These areas are generally practiced under family law or domestic relations.

Court Appointed Attorney

In some instances, if you cannot afford an attorney, you may be able to ask the judge to appoint you one for free. If this applies to you, take advantage of the opportunity. This is usually done at the first court appearance. In any event, I strongly suggest that you read as many chapters in this book as you can before meeting with your lawyer.

Using a lawyer for a limited purpose

1. Consultation
2. Review documents
3. Negotiate settlement

Full-scale legal representation may not be necessary or affordable. In such instances, you can always hire an attorney for limited purposes, such as: to consult with you and to explain legal documents or to clarify legal issues in your case; to explain your rights and liabilities; to allow you a second opinion on your case; or to give you a legal perspective that can enable you to represent yourself.

In certain situations, you may want to hire a lawyer for the limited purpose of negotiating a settlement in order to avoid going through a lengthy expensive trial. Keep in mind that if you decide to represent yourself but later change your mind, it may cost you more money in the end to have an attorney straighten out your matter than if you had hired an attorney from the start.

Meeting with an attorney

Before making an appointment to come in, find out if the lawyer offers a free consultation. If so, great! Take advantage of this opportunity to screen the lawyer to see just what your needs are. Keep in mind the need to scrutinize the attorney. When you walk into the lawyer's office, check out the lawyer's diplomas and certificates. See where and when the lawyer graduated from school. This will give you some idea of how long the attorney has been practicing. Also, you can check out the attorney before you meet with him or her by going to your public library and looking the person up in a lawyer's directory. There is one directory called **Martindale Hubbell**. You can also go online to look up attorneys. After you introduce yourself, the lawyer may take over and ask you basic questions like your name, address, and other background information. Then the attorney may ask you certain questions about your income and employment, or the attorney may ask you to talk, and then interrupt you with questions.

Say the attorney asks you to go first or gets through her questions and then asks you if you have any questions. Where do you begin? I would start with, "How long have you been practicing law? Do you specialize in family law?"
Just because someone goes to law school doesn't mean (s)he can practice any area of law. Ask if the lawyer is familiar with the court and judge in your case? Then ask the attorney to explain to you the child support guidelines.

But before you do this, I strongly recommend you read the rest of this chapter. Pay close attention to the section on what to bring your attorney as well as the chapter on child support. If it is custody or visitation you are after, read those chapters as well. This way you can ask any specific questions and test your attorney's knowledge of the subject matter. Again, just because a person went to law school doesn't make her/him a good lawyer. Ask yourself, does the lawyer seem confident? Did (s)he explain things to you in a way that you could understand, or did (s)he go right over your head like a fast ball? After that, I'd ask the attorney what do I need to prepare for court, what is the likelihood of trial, what would a trial entail, and how much could it cost?

Then, my next questions would be about legal fees. Find out what the lawyer charges and payment arrangements.

As you ask questions, you begin to see how well the lawyer is on top of the subject. Remember, there is no substitute for experience. More important, you will be able to check out the attorney's demeanor. How is (s)he coming across? Is (s)he loud and aggressive? Is (s)he quiet and reserved? Is (s)he friendly toward you? Ask yourself: am I comfortable with this person?

If the attorney constantly answers the telephone and gets distracted and preoccupied, (s)he may be too busy for you. Go to more than one attorney and take advantage of free consultations so you can compare attorneys. Keep in mind that each lawyer has a different style and a different expertise.

If you really want to test a new lawyer, show him/her this chapter. If (s)he agrees, you're in good hands. If (s)he says, "Wow, that's really interesting," find a lawyer with more experience. If you are interested in seeking custody and visitation, don't forget to ask the attorney if (s)he handles custody and visitation cases. Also ask if that attorney ever won custody for a father.

Once you've found a lawyer who looks as though (s)he may be able to help you, you are not off the hook.

It's your responsibility to work with your lawyer. Unlike magicians, lawyers cannot give you specific results. They represent you based on what you tell them. The better prepared you are, the easier your case will go and the more likely you are to save enormous time and money. The best way to work with your lawyer is by what I call the Three C's.

1. Communicate

Talk to your lawyer. Tell the truth. Open and honest communication is the best way to avoid misunderstandings about your case. During the course of your case, you may be tempted to vent your anger and frustration or to seek personal advice. It is not a good idea to use your time and money to call your lawyer just to vent—especially if it is about things the lawyer or the court can't do anything about.

Most lawyers are not always able to take every client's telephone calls right away. Many lawyers are very busy with trials or meetings. Most attorneys can and will return telephone calls if they want answers to specific questions. It's better to call your lawyer with specific questions, even to write them down for your lawyer to review and get back to you.

2. Compensate

Pay your bill. It always helps! A lawyer's fees vary with the level of experience. Some lawyers charge a flat fee while others require a retainer or an advance on fees. If the attorney completes the case for an amount less than the retainer, the attorney should return the unused portion of the fee.

Most lawyers charge on an hourly basis. Some charge different hourly rates for going to court and for working in their offices. In-court rates are usually higher than out-of-court rates. Either way you choose, make sure you get a written fee agreement detailing the services that will be covered.

3. Cooperate

In order to best assist your attorney in representing you in your child support case, you must provide him/her with all the necessary information about your case. Having the following documents handy makes this a cinch.

1. Income Tax Returns;
2. Bank Records;
3. Pay Stubs;
4. W-2 Forms;
5. Credit card statements;
6. List of insurance policies—life, auto, home, health and disability;
7. Deeds to real estate or apartment leases;
8. Divorce decrees and settlement agreements;
9. Other child support orders;
10. Receipts for child support payments.

* These items should also be found in the Financial Records section of your Court File.

For a lawyer, "Time Is Money"

When a lawyer is not in court representing clients, (s)he may spend time in the office reviewing documents, researching, planning strategy, talking to witnesses or to opposing counsel, drafting letters or preparing papers to file with the court.
Remember, your attorney's role is to provide calm, reasoned and detached advice in a diligent manner; it is not to help you seek revenge against the other party.

The Return Date

When you return to court, the judge will ask you to admit or deny

35

the allegations in the petition. If we are talking about paternity, this means that you are asked to admit or deny that you are the father of the subject child. If you are not married to the child's mother and you have any reason to doubt paternity, do not admit paternity. This is very serious. Don't just say, "Yes, I'm the father," to get the case over with. You must be absolutely sure you are the biological father. I've heard from many men who, believing that they were the father made the mistake of admitting paternity at the arraignment only to discover years later that they were not the biological father.

Notes:

Notes:

5

Paternity

Mamma's baby, Daddy's maybe?

It is one thing to say that you are the father and another thing to prove it, especially when a child is born and the parents are not married. In such cases, paternity must be established before a child support, visitation or custody order can be made. **Paternity is established when a court determines the legal father of a child.**

Who can bring a paternity suit?

Although under the law, either parent may bring a paternity suit, the mother usually brings a paternity petition against a man she claims to be the father of her child. A paternity suit is sometimes called a Filiation Hearing or an Establishment Hearing. A child's next of kin, the child, or a social services agency may also bring a paternity action. Establishing paternity can take up to one year in procedural delays.

Can a mother in another state claim me as the father?

Mothers can claim paternity against a father who resides in a different state. States have an arrangement that enables the CSEA to aid the mother in proving paternity even if the putative (alleged) father lives in a different state.

How is paternity established?

Establishing paternity involves the steps taken to verify the biological relationship between a child and the alleged father. There are several ways paternity can be established. In many states, there is a legal presumption that if you were married to the mother when the child was born or conceived, you are viewed as the legal father until proven otherwise. For example, in California, the presumption of paternity between married parents is indisputable. That means that if one of the married parents has an affair, although there are two potential fathers, the paternity of that child cannot be challenged. Some states like Iowa permit a presumed father to challenge paternity if he does so within certain time limits allowed by law.

For a newborn baby

A father can establish paternity voluntarily by signing a written acknowledgement of paternity at the time the baby is born and/or while the mother is still in the hospital. However, bear in mind that merely listing a father's name on the birth certificate does not by itself establish paternity. Since a father is not obligated to sign the birth certificate, a mother can list anyone she believes is the father of her child. Usually, both parents will sign the acknowledgment in front of a notary public. Once that is done and the voluntary acknowledgment of paternity is signed, it is filed in the district where the child was born. In some states, after 60 days or less, that acknowledgment becomes a finding of paternity. In other words, once the paternity acknowledgement is signed according to state law, it becomes permanent; you cannot change it, no matter what.

For an older child

You can go into court and file a request for an Order of Filiation to establish paternity regarding an older child. This happens often when unmarried parents separate and sue for custody over their children.

What can paternity do for me?

In addition to establishing child support orders, paternity is important because it shows that you respect your child enough to acknowledge that you are the legal father. On the other hand, paternity also creates and establishes a child's legal rights and privileges regarding inheritance and benefits, such as life insurance and medical benefits, social security benefits, veterans' benefits and military allowances, and right of inheritance. There may come a time when your child may be diagnosed with a certain disease that might be considered hereditary; in that case, it may be critical for your child to know the family's medical history for treatment purposes.

Paternity is also important because a child has a right to know who and where his parents are. Once paternity is established, a child is able to gain a sense of family identity and self-esteem. That child now has an opportunity to foster a relationship with the father and all those other relatives on the father's side of the family.

As a child's father, paternity gives you legal rights as a parent. It enables you to have your name on your child's birth certificate. It also protects your right to be notified in adoption proceedings for the child. Paternity is also the necessary first step in pursuing your right to custody or visitation.

Should I bring a paternity suit?

Before bringing a paternity suit, consider the following: Joe was the only father Devon had ever known. He took him out to the park, played ball, etc. For his sixth birthday, Joe bought Devon a bicycle. Devon called Joe, Daddy. Joe always had suspicions about Karen, Devon's mother, but he never followed up until one day Joe decided to confront Karen. Here, Joe must weigh the cost of how Devon will be affected by his actions. If Joe found out that Devon was not his son, the effects could be devastating, especially on Devon. Fortunately for Joe, Devon was his biological son. After Joe filed and established paternity, the parents were able to bring closure to the issue and strengthen their commitment to raising their son. Yes, fathers can file for paternity too. You may be a father who wants to have a relationship with his children but the custodial mother doesn't want to have anything to do with you. She denies you access to the children and even refuses your offer to pay support. In this case, to gain access to your child, you can file a paternity petition against a custodial mother to establish legal fatherhood.

What if I am not sure the child is mine?

If you have reason to believe the child in question is not yours, then do not sign the Acknowledgment of Paternity form. More importantly, do not admit paternity during your arraignment in court. This is especially important if the mother has had many sex partners, or if you believe that you are innocent and want to clear your name. You have the right to deny and challenge paternity or bring your own paternity suit. A paternity suit may be brought by either parent to have a court decide who the legal father of a child is. In some states, you may be able to contest paternity up to at least 18 years after a child is born. Nine times out of ten, it will be the mother suing the father for paternity in order to establish child support, with the father contesting paternity. Either way, if you challenge

41

paternity, you will have to appear in court and the mother will have to prove that you are the father of the child before you can be ordered to pay child support.

Paternity Tests

If you contest paternity, the court will order you, the mother, and the child to submit to a paternity test in order to establish the biological father. A paternity test compares the genetic markers from samples taken from the mother, the child and the alleged father. The court will then consider the tests and other evidence to determine whether or not you are legally the father of the child. Where the tests reveal the probability of paternity, 95% or higher, you are presumed to be the child's father. When this happens, the burden of proof shifts to you to prove that you are not the father of that child.

Another way to establish paternity

Hearing

A court may hold a hearing where witnesses can testify about the parties and the circumstances surrounding the birth of the child. A judge will look at the evidence and decide that there is enough evidence to make a finding of paternity. The main evidence a judge considers is the paternity test results. At times, a judge may hear the person from the laboratory who testifies about the test results. S(h)ewill be considered an expert witness.

Paternity by conduct

In some states, under the Uniform Parentage Act (UPA 1973), if a man receives a child into his home and assumes responsibility for that child and raises it as his own, the law deems him to be the child's father.

Do I need a lawyer? What if I can't afford one?

You have a right to have an attorney to help you during the paternity hearing. If you cannot afford an attorney, ask the court to appoint you one.

How much do these tests cost and who pays for them?

These tests can be expensive. The average cost of such blood tests ranges from $200 to $400. If, after the tests, you are found to be the father, you may be held responsible to pay for the cost of the tests. If so, you probably won't be able to reduce the amount, but you may be able to make arrangements to pay in installments. If a mother is receiving benefit payments from Aid to Families of Dependent Children (AFDC--welfare), the father pays only if the tests prove his paternity.

What if I am not the father?

The tests will show if you are not the child's father. If so, then the court will dismiss the case and you will be relieved of your obligation to pay child support. Keep in mind that these tests are very accurate and the results are hard to disprove. Courts rely heavily on paternity tests. So, challenging paternity tests just to buy time can be a waste of time and money.

What if I am the father?

If the court determines that you are the father, the court will give you a legal document known as an Order of Filiation. Once this is done, you are now legally recognized as the child's father and have all the rights and responsibilities of a parent in the same manner accorded you if you were married. The court can now determine how much you will have to pay for child support.

What is temporary child support?

During the time your support case is pending, a Support Magistrate must issue a child support order temporarily in an amount sufficient to meet the needs of the child, even if your income and asset information is not available.

Once a temporary support order is made, the Support Magistrate or Hearing Officer will usually give you another date to return to court (return date) on the child support case. Before you leave the courtroom, the court officer will usually hand you a notice to appear in court. That notice will tell you the date, time and name of the Support Magistrate you are to appear before. It will also tell you what papers to bring with you when you come back on the return date. You may be told to bring the following:

1. W-2's;
2. Income Tax Returns;
3. Statement of Net Worth;
4. Most recent pay stubs.

Before you leave the courtroom, make sure you ask the Support Magistrate for a copy of the child support guidelines used by the court. If you are not represented by an attorney, the court must give you a copy. That will give you an idea about how much you will have to pay. I will explain in more detail later. Meanwhile, let's get ready for court.

Notes:

Notes:

6

Getting Organized

How to set up a Court File

If you are like a lot people, you are probably not good at keeping records. Have you ever forgotten about your court papers or waited until the last minute, and you mistakenly missed your court date and ended up in jail on a bench warrant? If this sounds familiar, then you are not alone. Like many others, you may lack the necessary organizational skills to get through the system.

In order to deal with the family court system, you have to be very organized. You must keep all of your records and documents that relate to your case in one place. One way to do this is to set up a file containing all of the items that you will need to bring to court. It's not hard at all. I'll show you a few simple tips to keep your papers in order and to be ready for court too. If there is one part of this book I hope you will use, it is this one. The techniques discussed in this chapter will teach you how to get organized. Sound simple? It is. Let's get started.

First, you will need the following supplies:

1. **Pens**: Keep several pens handy. They are a must-have for court, so you can take notes and sign papers;

2. **Paperclips**: You will use these to keep your papers together;

3. **One (1) Large Folder**: Get one that opens and closes like an envelope; mark it "Court File." You will use this folder to house all of your documents and files;

4. **Six (6) Letter sized manila file folders**: You will use these to separate your court papers into categories. In the next section, I will show you how;

5. **Notepaper**: You will use this to write letters to the court, to the CSEA, etc;

6. **Letter envelopes and postage stamps**: You will use these to send letters or information and/or child support payments;

7. **Small notepad journal**: the small notebook comes in handy as a journal to take down notes about your case in, and out of court. You can keep notes on missed visits and incidents;

8. **Calculator**: A calculator is necessary to add up amounts to figure out your child support payments;

9. **Calendar**: This is a very important item. Your calendar can be used to mark payments, court dates, etc. You can either get a calendar book or a wall calendar.

In addition, you can use your calendar as a reference guide to keep track of scheduled visitations/parenting time, denied visitations and telephone calls, etc. It is also very useful during a hearing to recall important dates.

The Next Nine Steps to follow

Step 1: Take five letter-sized manila file folders. Mark the first folder "Contacts." This is where you will keep important telephone numbers and addresses for the court and lawyers, accountants and the support collection unit. Important information to have at your fingertips is the judge's name, courtroom and case number. You will also include a communication log in this file. It may be necessary to remember to whom you spoke, when and what you discussed.

Example: Telephone Log
Case number_____

Person Called_____
Telephone number_____
Date_____ Time_____

Contact made: Yes   No

Message left: Yes   No

Reason for telephone call:

_____

_____

_____

Returned call received: date_____ time_____

Results: _____

_____

_____

Action to be taken:

_____

_____

_____

Follow up on: _____

(For a sample telephone log, see Appendix F.)

Step 2: Mark the second folder "Court Papers."

This file will store all of the child support orders, summonses and petitions, and any other documents you receive from the court. Remember to check the postmarks and certificates of service on all papers against the actual date(s) you received them. There are certain time limits for which court papers have to be served on you.

Step 3: Mark the third folder "Financial Information."

This is where you will keep all of your income and expense information, like your pay stubs, tax returns and W-2's. Make sure to photocopy these documents before you put them in the file. You will need to present many of these documents in court. Courts usually do not return documents; so if you give them originals, make sure you have photocopies.

Step 4: Mark the forth folder "Child Support Payments."

This is where you will keep a payment log in addition to your receipts or cancelled checks. It serves as proof of payment. Remember-- never ever send cash; there is no way to prove that you paid. If the mother denies receiving payment, you will have to pay her again. This is also where you will keep your child support collection statements.

Step 5: Mark the fifth folder "Access and Parenting Time."

This file is used to document your access to (visitation with) your children.

Step 6: Now take out your small notebook and your calculator. Place these items in the large folder in front of the four manila folders so that you can easily get to it. Your notebook comes in handy as a journal to take down notes about your case in and out of court. And you will also have your calculator handy to add up numbers and child support amounts. Make sure to put some pens in the folder too.

Step 7: Now take out your Calendar. This is a very important item. Your calendar can be used to mark payments, court dates, and appointments with lawyers, accountants and support collection agents. In addition, you can use your calendar as a reference guide to keep track of scheduled visitations, denied visitations and telephone calls. It is also very useful during a hearing to recall important dates. Place your calendar behind the four folders.

Step 8: Now take out your notepaper, envelopes and postage stamps. Put these items behind your calendar. You will use these items for writing letters or sending child support payments.

Congratulations, you have now set up your court file. You will bring this file with you to court. Your court file keeps all of your important information together and comes in handy during hearings. However, to make your court file complete, you must prepare a Statement of Net Worth.

In order for the court to set the amount of child support that you will pay, both parents will have to complete financial statements detailing their respective monthly income and expenses. This gives the court a clear picture of both parents' financial situation. This form is very important.

The law requires you to complete a sworn Statement of Net Worth. If you do not complete this statement, the court can, on its own, grant the petitioner the relief demanded in the petition, or for purposes of the child support proceeding, preclude you from offering any evidence to show your financial ability to pay child support. In other words, if you don't complete and file this form with the court, the Support Magistrate or Hearing Officer can rule against you and order an amount of child support, and you won't be able to object. To show you how to fill in the forms, I have inserted the part of the form that applies for each instruction. Be sure to follow these instructions carefully. (You will find a sample Net

Worth Statement in Appendix G.)

Step 9: Preparing your Statement of Net Worth Now take out your file folder marked "Financial Information." Find the following:

1. Current pay-stubs;
2. W-2's;
3. Last year's income tax return.

Photocopy these documents. Now, go to the "Statement of Net Worth." Complete the Preliminary Information Section in Part 1(A). Then proceed from there to fill out each subsequent section.

Part I (A). Preliminary Information:

Employment Status: Self –employed [] Yes [] No
Employer: _____
Address: _____
Hrs. per week: _____ Pay period _____ Rate of pay_____
Number of children   _____
Names   Ages   Reside with you? _____

_____   _____   _____
_____   _____   _____
_____   _____   _____
_____   _____   _____

Now, go to Part B Income. Review your pay-stubs carefully. Transfer the amounts from your pay-stubs onto each of the following columns and calculate total. Transfer the amount of income you declared on your tax return.

Part I (B). Income Information:
Gross (weekly) Salary earned last year: $_____
Social Security $_____
Federal Tax $_____
State Tax $_____
Medicare: $_____
FICA $_____
Other Payroll deductions:
_____ $_____

Net Weekly Salary $_____

      Part-time job $_____

      Pension $_____

      Retirement $_____

      Unemployment $_____ $_____

      Disability $_____

      Rental income $_____

      Bonuses $_____

      Commissions $_____

Other income: $_____

Total Weekly Income $_____ $_____

Income declared on last year's

Federal Tax Return $_____

Next, Go to Part II: Assets.

     Gather your rent or mortgage statements, bank account statements, cancelled checks, automobile information, etc. Complete Part II. Calculate totals.

Part II. Assets:

Residence owned [ ] Yes   [ ]No

Address_____

Estimated Market Value $_____

Mortgage owed $_____

Other Real Property Owned: [ ] Yes   [ ] No

Address_____

Estimated Market Value $_____

Mortgage owed $_____

Savings Account balance $_____

Checking Account balance $_____

Stocks, bonds $_____

Money owed to you $_____

Retirement plans, IRA $_____

Profit sharing, pension, 401K $_____

Automobile   Value $_____

(Year)_____

(Make) _____

Boat, trailer, etc. $_____

_____

Other personal property $_____

_____

Total Assets: $_____

Next, go to Part III: Expenses.

To figure out your expenses, collect your bills, invoices, and statements. Make photocopies of the bills and clip them together. Now, take a yellow highlighter pen to highlight the totals on each bill or statement, like telephone bills and rent receipts, for example.

Note: Most courts consider reasonable expenses for your basic needs, like rent or mortgage, food and clothing, etc., over lifestyle choices, such as entertainment expenses (like dinning out, etc). If applicable, include any court-ordered child support payments for other children. Attach money order receipts or cancelled checks, receipts for clothing, and other items and costs that you have provided for your child.

Part III. Expenses: [ ] Monthly   [ ] Weekly
Rent [ ]   Mortgage [ ] $_____
Food: Self $_____
Children(school lunch) $_____
Utilities:
        Heat $_____
        Gas $_____
        Electric $_____
        Telephone $_____
        Heating fuel $_____
        Water $_____
        Garbage removal $_____
Total Utilities: $_____

Clothing: Self_____   Children_____ $_____
Laundry: Self_____   Children_____ $_____
Medical: Self_____   Children_____ $_____
Dental: Self_____   Children_____ $_____
Medication: Self_____   Children_____ $_____

Insurance:
Life_____   Auto_____   Fire_____ $_____
Health $_____   Accident $_____ $_____

Transportation:
Carfare $_____
Toll $_____
Gas/oil $_____
Maintenance $_____
Auto payment: $_____

Balance due
on loan $_____ $_____

Tuition: $_____ $_____
Other: $_____ $_____

Total Expenses $_____

After you have finished highlighting all your expenses on the receipts, make a summary sheet of all the amounts that you have calculated. Attach a summary sheet in front of the photocopies and clip them together. Then, transfer the total expenses to the net worth statement as indicated.

Now Go to Part IV Liabilities
Liabilities are things you are responsible for, like debts, loans, credit card balances, etc.

Make copies of the documents and statements and highlight the amounts due even if you haven't paid or are unable to pay them. A bill is a bill. It is still an amount owed.

Part IV. Liabilities: (Debts, loans, credit cards, etc.)
Owed to_____
Purpose_____
Date incurred_____   Balance due_____
                           Monthly payment $_____

Owed to_____

Purpose_____

Date incurred_____ Balance due_____

Monthly payment $_____

Owed to_____

Purpose_____

Date incurred_____ Balance due_____

Monthly payment $_____

Total Monthly Payments $_____

Now you are ready to calculate the net worth statement. Get your calculator. Add up all of the total amounts at the end of each part.

Make three copies of the Net Worth Statement. Keep one in your court file. One copy you will exchange with the other side. The third copy is for the court. Congratulations, you have completed your net worth statement. Next, we are going to learn about Child Support just before we go to court!

Notes:

Notes:

Notes:

7

About Child Support

Child support is not a payment you make in order to see your child!

As we discussed, Alimony is a separate issue. Paternity is a separate issue. Divorce is a separate issue. Visitation Rights/ Parenting Time are a separate issue. Even Custody is a separate issue. Issues of Visitation and Child support are not dependent upon each other. One cannot be viewed by either parent as something that is tied to the other, especially in a court of law. Each issue (each matter) that is brought before the court is handled separately. From a legal standpoint, when parents are separated, the parent who does not live with the child is supposed to make a regular payment of money to the parent who lives with the child in order to help raise and care for that child. That payment is called child support. The parent who lives with the child is also known as the custodial parent. Often, the custodial parent is the child's mother, but this isn't always true. Sometimes it's the child's grandmother or some other relative. It may also be the foster parent, the county or the state.

In addition to the regular payment of money, child support also refers to the cost for medical support, childcare, health insurance, unreimbursed health care expenses, and life insurance, education and after-school activities, as well as vacation expenses. A non-custodial parent may be ordered to provide medical insurance coverage for the child or make an additional payment toward insurance coverage or for health care expenses, such as therapy, dental, orthodontic, etc.

Child support can also take the form of a family support order. For example, in a divorce case where the custodial parent gets to stay in the house with the children until they reach the age of majority, the non-custodial parent could be made to pay the mortgage and taxes through a family support order.

Who pays child support?

The person who takes care of the child from day to day needs money to help provide food, clothing, shelter and basic necessities for the child. So, courts order either or both parents to pay the person who has that responsibility. States have enacted guidelines to determine support. The amount that must be paid is determined by a series of factors: how much income each of the parties earns or has the ability to earn, in addition to how much it costs to adequately support that child, etc. There may be factors that are considered in making an award of support that are different from the guidelines order.

In the eyes of the law, both parents have a duty to financially support their children, no matter what. However, the law presumes that the custodial parent is already paying a fair share of child support. Therefore, if you are the parent who does not live with your child, you are known as the non-custodial parent. Under the child support laws, you are the one who has to pay child support. Since mothers more often that not get custody of the children, I will refer to them in this book as the "custodial parent." That is not to say that fathers cannot get custody. Fathers can and do win custody.

However, since this book focuses on fathers who have to pay child support, I will refer to mothers as custodial parents who receive child support and to fathers as non-custodial parents who pay child support.

What if I am not married to my child's mother?

It doesn't matter if you were never married to your child's mother. Your duty to support your child begins when your child is born and continues until your child reaches adulthood or the legal equivalent (what is called "the age of majority"). The age of legal adulthood differs in various states. As the divorce rate and out-of-wedlock birth rates steadily climb, the issue of child support is becoming a fact of life for many. If you are a father of a child born out of wedlock, chances are you will experience a child support proceeding.

For a child born to parents who are married to each other, the husband is presumed to be the legal father and is responsible for providing child support on behalf of that child. However, when parents are separated or divorced, a court tries to enforce a child's right to financial support by setting up a child support order.

For a child born out of wedlock, paternity (legal fatherhood) must be established before a child support order is made (see Chapter Three, Paternity).

Can fathers claim child support from mothers?

If you are a father who has custody, you are entitled to seek child support. Remember, both parents have a duty to support their children regardless of gender. Child support is not gender specific. Child support is payable to the parent who has custody. In other words, child support is not automatically payable to the mother. That means that if a father has custody of the children, he can file for child support against the mother. Under the law, the court can enforce the order against the non-custodial mother the same way it can enforce the order against you, if she has custody.

What if I have no income?

If you do not have income, and you are receiving public assistance, or if you are ordered to pay the standard amount that would place you below the poverty level, the Support Magistrate may not make a support order or may reduce the order to a lower amount. Make sure you inform the Support Magistrate of your situation.

What are alimony, maintenance, and spousal support?

Alimony in some states, such as New York, is called maintenance. It's money paid to a spouse to maintain the standard of living that was established during the marriage.

In order to help a spouse provide for her own reasonable needs, the court will look at certain factors, such as the duration of the marriage, the present and future earning capacity of the parties, the ability of the party seeking maintenance to become self-supporting, and the other spouse's resources and ability to pay the alimony.

In New York, the issues of child support and maintenance are interrelated. Before child support is calculated, spousal support, maintenance and alimony paid are subtracted from the income of the payer.

The distinction between alimony and child support is that the first is paid on behalf of the spouse; the second is paid on behalf of the child. Both, by the way, are separate issues and would, in all probability, be discussed and resolved separately. One does not automatically come with the other. It depends on what issue (what matter) is before the court. If a spouse is suing for alimony and child support, then the judge may rule on both. If the matter before the court is only that of child support, then the court will make a determination only with regard to child support. Only the custodial parent can sue for child support. Since each spouse is supposed to support the other, either spouse can sue for alimony.

Can my child's mother and I make our own agreement?

Both you and your child's mother can agree that you will pay a certain amount of child support without the involvement of the court. This is okay as long as you both stick to it. This form of agreement is known as "settling (a matter) out of court." However, for this agreement to be binding, it will have to be approved by a court. This requires an oral agreement before the court set forth in an order or a written agreement submitted to the court. Some states, including New York, require the order to be in compliance with the child support guidelines or to have the reasons why it is not in compliance set forth. That means, once you have a written agreement, you must go to court and obtain a court order. Otherwise, your agreement will not be enforceable in a court of law. Just remember to keep records of what you paid, so that if you ever have to go to court, you can get credit for your payments. If you give cash (which you should never do), make sure that you get a signed receipt from her. Otherwise, you will have no way of proving that you paid her. She can always say you didn't pay her, and you may end up having to pay her again.

Are you thinking about making your own child support agreement?

Here are some questions to consider:

1. How much would you pay under your state's guidelines?
2. What does the child need?
3. What are your financial resources?
4. What are the mother's financial resources?
5. What are the healthcare expenses and who will pay them?
6. What are the educational expenses and who will pay them?
7. Who will provide health insurance for the child?
8. What other expenses will be considered?
9. Who will take the tax exemption?
10. How much will you pay?
11. How and when will payments be made?
12. Will there be a trust, life insurance or other forms of security along with or to guarantee the payments?

How much do I have to pay?

In order to determine the amount of child support you will actually pay, the judge or Support Magistrate will use Child Support Guidelines. These guidelines were developed under the Federal Child Support Enforcement Act of 1984. Now every state must follow a set of guidelines that consist of numerical formulas for determining child support. These formulas were based on studies of how much money families ordinarily spend for raising a child. The guidelines take into consideration the amount of income a family would have spent to support a child if the parties were not separated. Keep in mind that child support is not the same in every state (or in every county). Each state and county calculates child support differently and has its own set of guidelines. In New York, the guidelines are applicable in all counties. Still, most child support guidelines consider the needs of the child, such as medical insurance, education, day care, special needs, other dependents, as well as the income that both parties earn and the non-custodial parent's ability to pay.

Some guidelines look only at the income of the person who will be paying child support, while other states look at the combined income of both parents. Since the amounts of child support are already fixed within the guidelines, all the decision maker really has to do is plug in your income to the formula to come up with the amount of support you owe or will be expected and ordered to pay.

Determining the Guideline Amount

In order to figure out how much you will have to pay, it is a good idea to get a copy of the child support guidelines currently being used by the court in your jurisdiction before your scheduled court date. Reviewing the guidelines ahead of time takes the mystery out of what you could or would be ordered to pay. These guidelines are easy to get. You can either go to Family Court or ask the court clerk for a copy. You could also contact the child support enforcement office, or you can ask a family lawyer. Guidelines are available at all public libraries. Now, you can even go online at "http://www.childsupportguidelines.com to get a copy of those guidelines.

Types of Guidelines

There are roughly three different child support models used in various states.

The income shares model is based on the income of both parents and the number of children. For example, let's say that the mother has custody of the two children. She earns $10,000 per year and you earn $30,000 per year. To make it easy, let's assume that these are all the net amounts and there are no further deductions or adjustments.

The Support Magistrate or judge will add both of your incomes.

Mom's income	$10,000	25%	+
Dad's income	$30,000	75%	=
Combined parental income	$40,000	100%	

Next, the Support Magistrate will look at the child support guidelines to determine the total child support obligation of each parent (or the obligation of the parent being sued).

NUMBER OF CHILDREN

Annual Income	one	two	three	four	five+
20,000	3,400	5,000	5,800	6,200	7,000
25,000	4,250	6,250	7,250	7,750	8,750
30,000	5,100	7,500	8,700	9,300	10,500
35,000	5,950	8,750	10,150	10,850	12,250
40,000	6,800	**10,000**	11,600	12,400	14,000

Here, the total child support obligation would be $10,000 per year. Now, the judge or Support Magistrate must determine each parent's share of the combined income.

Mom's income	$10,000	25%	+
Dad's income	$30,000	75%	=
Combined income	$40,000	100%	

The combined income is divided between you and the other parent in proportion to your income.

Mom	$2,500	25%	+
Dad	**$7,500**	**75%**	=
	$10,000	100%	

64

Now, the judge or Support Magistrate orders you to pay 75% or $7,500 per year to the mother. Since the mother has custody, she is presumed to be paying her share. So she is not ordered to pay her 25% or $2,500. (For a list of states that use the income shares model see Appendix C.)

A second model is the **Percentage of Income Model** It is used to calculate support based on a percentage of your income (either as gross or net) against the number of children.

Children   **% of Net Income**

(Child Support Percentages of
Combined parental income)

One child	17%
Two children	25%
Three children	29%
Four children	31%
Five children	

No less than 35% of combined parental income).

Here, the judge or Support Magistrate locates the child support percentage based on the amount of children. Then the judge or Support Magistrate applies the percentage to your income.

Dad's income $4,000 x 25% =
% (Percentage) of income   **$1,000**

Now, the judge or Support Magistrate orders you to pay $1,000. (For a list of states that use the percent of income model see Appendix C.)

The Melson Formula is named after Judge Elwood F. Melson of the Delaware Family Court. This model is used only in a few states. It takes into consideration the financial needs of the parents in addition to the child's financial needs. It then factors in childcare and other extraordinary medical expenses. Then a standard of living allowance is determined. (For a list of states that use the Melson formula, see Appendix C.)

What Else Does the Court Consider?

Children's Expenses

In addition to the costs of raising a child (i.e., food, clothing and shelter), children incur other expenses. In making a child support order, the court typically considers the following expenses: health insurance, health care expenses, education tuition, tutors, books, and fees, childcare and babysitting, costs of extracurricular activities (such as sports, equipment, uniforms and hobbies).

Departing from the Guidelines

There is a presumption in the law that the amount of child support calculated under the guidelines is the correct amount. For that reason, Support Magistrates are reluctant to depart from the child support guidelines. Remember, guidelines apply in divorce cases too! But that does not mean that the amount cannot be challenged. You or the other parent can challenge the amount by offering evidence to show that the amount ordered is not correct. If the judge or Support Magistrate finds that the amount ordered under the guidelines is "unjust or inappropriate," you may be ordered to pay a different amount than what the guidelines require. If this happens, the Support Magistrate must set forth its reasons in writing as part of the official record. Either party may object to the Support Magistrate's findings.

Here are some reasons for support being granted above the guidelines:

1. Special education needs, like tutoring or speech therapy;
2. Childcare expenses;
3. Medical-dental expenses not covered by insurance;
4. Recreation-summer camp, sports, after-school activities;
5. The resources of the non-custodial parent are substantially greater than the custodial parent;
6. The tax benefits to the non-custodial parent;
7. The educational needs of the custodial parent;
8. Voluntary unemployment or underemployment;
9. You remarry and your new spouse has income that contributes to that household in such a way that it frees up your funds, which factor now enables you to pay

Here are some reasons for awarding support that is less than below the guidelines:

1. Joint Custody or situations where your children spend an equal amount of time with each parent;

2. Split Custody or situations where the children are split between the parents (for example, the son goes to live with the father while the daughter lives with the mother);

3. Other child support obligations for other children of the former spouse;

4. Other maintenance or spousal support obligations;

5. Resources of the children, i.e., trust funds;

6. Tax benefits to the custodial parent;

7. Your income is so high that applying the guidelines would result in child support order that is higher than the child's reasonable needs.

Calculating Child Support

In order to calculate child support, you will need a calculator.

First, check the guidelines to find out what is included and excluded from gross income. In some states, the guidelines allow certain deductions from gross income before establishing the amount of income that will be used to determine child support. (See if your state uses Gross Income or Net Income. Gross income is the total amount you earn before deductions are made. Net Income is the total amount you earn after deductions are made.)

Inclusions

For child support purposes, Income includes any earned, unearned, taxable or nontaxable income, benefits or periodic lump sum payments due to you, regardless of source. Courts take into account your income from all sources, including but not limited to:

1. Wages, bonuses, commissions, overtime and tips;

2. Dividends, retirement plan;

3. Distributions, annuities;

4. Interest income;

5. Royalties;

6. Trust income;

7. Capital gains;

8. Rental income;

9. Gifts, prizes;

10. Maintenance, alimony or spousal support;

11. Unemployment, workers' compensation;

12. Disability benefits;
13. Social Security;
14. Severance pay;
15. Pensions.

Some states include the income of other household members.

Each state has its own allowable deductions. These are usually mandatory payments you must make, for example:

1. Withholding for federal and state taxes;
2. Mandatory union dues;
3. Business expenses for self-employed persons;
4. Social security (FICA);
5. Dependent exemptions;
6. State disability insurance (SDI);
7. Mandatory retirement contributions;
8. Children's health insurance;
9. Prior child support.

Some guidelines use gross income, while others use net income.

Gross income
Gross income is all the money you received before tax income expenses. The court will then subtract certain expenses that are already allowed by law, resulting in "adjusted" gross income.

Adjusted Gross Income
Deductions: After the Adjusted Gross Income is determined; the court may subtract certain other deductions allowed by law.

Net income
This is your net income by which child support payments will be determined.

1. **Look up the guidelines used in your jurisdiction to see what types of income can be deducted.**

2. **Now, check to see if there is a different rate or an adjustment for a father who has a lot of extended parenting time (visitation).** The difference in rate is based on the idea that the more time you spend with

your children, the less money you will have to pay in child support for food, clothing and shelter. Some states allow a 50% reduction of child support when a father has consecutive parenting time for a certain amount of days, or overnights, usually more than seven days a month. If this applies to you, make sure that this provision is included in your child support order.

3. **You may also be able to have the costs of transporting the children during parenting time (visitation) offset your child support obligation rather than treating it as a deduction.**
Example: Let's say that, in order to transport your children for the purposes of visitation, you travel 115 miles per week for 45 weeks @ $.22 per mile, totaling $ 1,138.50 per year. This amount can be deducted from the total payment to the mother.

4. **Check to see if certain receipts, such as public assistance, food stamps and gifts, are totally or partially excluded from the court's determination.**

5. **Next, find out whether there are adjustments you can ask for in situations that include other children from a previous relationship.** If you are already paying child support, you may be able to deduct the amount of child support you pay for the other children from your net income, and thus reduce the amount of child support for the child(ren) in question. There are usually two requirements:
   a. The child support for the other children must be court ordered;
   b. You are actually paying it.

6. **Find out if alimony is deductible.**

7. **Find out if there are adjustments for overtime or seasonal employment.** Some states may consider certain job expenses, like maintaining a car or the cost for special work clothes. While other expenses, like credit card debt or ordinary house hold expenses are usually not considered, courts may consider extraordinary expenses like medical bills.
Commonly Asked Questions

Can I deduct child support from my taxes?
No. Child support is not deductible by the payer nor is it viewed as taxable to the recipient.

Can I claim my child as a dependent if I am paying child support?
Both parents may not claim the same child as a tax exemption. Generally, the parent who has custody over the child for the longest part

of the year gets to claim the exemption. The father may be able to take the exemption in situations where the mother has physical custody but the father pays over 50% of the child's support, provided that he files an IRS Form 8332 (Release of Claim to Exemption for Child of Divorced or Separated Parents) that is also signed by the mother.

Do I still have to pay child support if I file bankruptcy?

Yes. Child support cannot be discharged in bankruptcy.

What if I am living in another state? Do I still have to pay child support?

Yes. Under the Uniform Interstate Family Support Act (UIFSA), child support orders are enforceable across state lines.

I am a full time student and not employed. Do I have to pay child support?

The judge or Support Magistrate may require you to find employment before or after school to provide some support. When you begin to earn, you will be required to pay support.

Do I still have to pay child support during the summer when my child spends vacation with me?

Yes. Full support is still due. Child support is based on expenses, such as rent, mortgage, utilities, clothes and insurance, which still have to be paid even when the child is away on summer vacation. However, you and your child's mother are free to arrange between yourselves different payment arrangements when the child is with you.

What if I am in the military?

Members of the armed services are still liable for their child support obligation. Under the Uniform Code of Military Justice, a parent-soldier can face punitive measures if s(h)e fails to pay. However, the Soldiers' and Sailors' Relief Act does provide for temporary stays under certain circumstances. For more information on child support and the military visit the following websites:

www.acf.hhs.gov/programs/cse/
www.jagnet.army.mil/Legal

Other factors that affect child support.

There are several other factors the court may consider that could affect child support. For example, one parent may have very high income and the child support guidelines may have calculated more than what the child needs. Here, the court would have a basis to deviate from the guidelines.

Courts may also consider cases where the father would not have enough money to live. Say that the mother remarries and her husband makes good money. Some states may consider the income of the new spouse and adjust child support accordingly, while other states may not.

Are you self-employed?

Parents who are self-employed must keep accurate records. Self-employed individuals are heavily scrutinized because they can easily manipulate their books to reveal a "loss on paper" while maintaining a comfortable standard of living. If this applies to you, beware. The CSEA can obtain copies of your credit report to figure out your true income. If you fail to keep accurate records, your child support obligation may be calculated on the basis of what the Support Magistrate thinks you earn instead of what you actually earn. As it relates to business expenses, remember, certain expenses that are tax deductible are not deductible for child support purposes. However, reasonable business expenses are deductible, though there may be limitations on depreciation. You may want to consider hiring an accountant or bookkeeper to help prepare your financial statements.

Once you have calculated your income level, check the guidelines to determine the amount of support you will have to pay at that income level.

Example: To find the yearly child support obligation, use the table below:

Annual Income	Number of Children				
	1	2	3	4	5+
$11,000-11,999	600	600	300	300	300
12,000-12,099	876	876	876	876	876

A father's child support obligation does not stop here. In addition to the fixed amount of your basic child support obligation, you can be ordered to pay unreimbursed health expenses, provide life insurance, provide medical insurance, and pay childcare. You may also be ordered to pay your share of the babysitting expenses as well as related educational expenses.

Notes:

Notes:

Notes:

8

The Child Support Hearing

(Please Note: the following information is intended to assist you during the crucial period known as the Hearing. This information may be helpful in showing you what to expect during the child support hearing process. Warning! Child support hearings can sometimes be very adversarial. If you have to go to court and you are not sure or are unclear about any of the information, contact an attorney.)

If you are scheduled for a hearing and you don't show up to the hearing, you are making a big mistake. The Support Magistrate can go ahead and make a child support order against you without knowing how much you really earn. The Support Magistrate can also set the arrears (back child support) from the date your child's mother filed the petition against you.

You must be present in court to show the Support Magistrate your financial situation so that you are not ordered to pay what the court thought you earned. As far as the law is concerned, that is what you owe. You will be held accountable for that amount. If you do not appear in court, the judge or Support Magistrate may also issue a warrant for your arrest and, in some instances, even suspend your driver's license. You can avoid these consequences by just showing up when you are supposed to, and with your Court File.

What do I bring to Court?

There is no truth without proof! When you go to court, don't forget to bring your Court File. You might want to keep your financial information in the front of your file, so you can get to it quicker. You will need to provide the court with all the documents that show your income. This includes income tax returns, pay stubs and net worth statement. Also, if you are paying child support for other children, bring records of payment for those orders from the support collection unit or, if payments are payable directly, bring copies of money orders or cancelled checks, and bring the orders. If you have been paying child support for the children in question since the date the petition was filed, bring proof of that too.

In addition to all cancelled checks, money order receipts bring all other receipts of payments made for health insurance, childcare, health-care, educational expenses, and clothing that you purchased for the children in question. If you are self–employed, bring proof of expenses to operate the business, such as rent, utilities, insurance, transportation, etc.

Bring all of the information that shows your expenses. These items may reduce your income level. Financial disclosure is extremely important because the Support Magistrate will use this information to determine what you will have to pay. If you do not give the court your financial information, the Support Magistrate can make what is known in the law as a negative inference against you and impute income. That means that the Support Magistrate can order child support based upon what (s)he thinks is your income. If this happens, you will not be able to object successfully to the child support order later.

During a hearing

1. Don't volunteer information during a hearing. Only answer the question asked. Volunteering information does not score any extra points.

2. Never storm out of the courtroom or leave without permission.

3. If you are asked a question and someone objects, wait for the judge to rule on the objection before you answer.

4. When the judge asks you a question, speak only to the court. Never turn and speak directly to your Ex or her attorney.

5. Watch your tone of voice. Don't get loud.

At the hearing, both parties appear before the judge or the Support Magistrate. The hearing is relatively informal. However, this does not mean that you should take the hearing lightly. The proceedings are usually recorded. The Support Magistrate listens to both sides of the case, taking sworn testimony about income, expenses and the cost of supporting the child. Both you and the other side can present evidence and witnesses, and you can cross-examine (question) the other party's witnesses.

The petitioner goes first and will usually be the only witness. He or she will testify as to the names and ages of the children, the income, expenses and the children's needs. If an attorney does not represent the respondent, then the Support Magistrate may question the respondent about his or her income and expenses. At the end of the hearing, the Support Magistrate will make a decision about how much you have to pay. A schedule for payments known as Child Support will be set or ordered upon you.

Under the law, you can be held responsible for paying child support from the date the petition was filed; this is called "retroactive child support." This is also another way arrears (back child support) are established. Since it could take months from the time paternity is established to make a final child support order, it is possible that your case could get adjourned (postponed) for months. Your child support order may very well tell you that you have to pay from the date the mother filed the child support petition against you, which is different from the date the child support order was made. In that case, you would owe retroactive child support in addition to each subsequent payment.

Notes:

Notes:

9

After the Hearing

After the child support hearing, the judge or Support Magistrate will sign the child support order, and you will get a copy. Make sure you read your order carefully. It should tell you how much you have to pay, when the payments start and where to send them.

How do I pay?
If you are working a job, more than likely the Child Support Enforcement Agency (CSEA) will send an income execution order to your employer. An income execution is a notice to your employer to take the money directly out of your paycheck. Your employer then sends the money to the CSEA, which, in turn, sends it to the mother. So, by the time you get your paycheck, your child support payment is already on its way to the mother. The CSEA also keeps records on how much you owe and how much you have paid.

If you are unemployed, or if you are self-employed, you will be responsible for sending your payments directly to the support collection agency by mail. Be careful! When you make your payment, if you send the CSEA your personal check, it will know where you bank and have your bank account number. If it happens that you owe back child support (arrears), you may find out that the money you thought you had is gone, without any warning.

Paying the mother directly
Sometimes you may be ordered to pay the mother directly without the CSEA getting involved. In this instance, record keeping is essential. There is a tendency among fathers to try to work things out with the child's mother if the two of you are getting along; it is easier to just give her the cash. But what happens when she changes her mind and things are

not working out? Now, you have given her the power, and you will end up getting the short end of the stick.

Whatever you do, never ever pay your child's mother in cash without getting a signed receipt from her. Otherwise, she can always say that you never paid her. A better way to avoid the drama and headaches is to pay her by money order and to keep all of your receipts. You may need them later in court to prove that you paid her when she claims otherwise. Otherwise, it will be your word against hers, and you may be ordered to pay her again.

Creating the account

When the Support Magistrate in Family Court makes an order payable through the CSEA, an account is created. You will be assigned a number to identify your account.

Under this account arrangement, you must make your payments directly to the Child Support Collection Unit (CSCU) according to the order. Remember to include your name and your social security number on your check or money order so that you are given credit for your payments.

You may receive payment coupons and a written Notice of Payment instructions detailing how and when to make your child support payments. This notice is very important, so keep it together with your other court documents in your Court File.

Example: SUPPORT PAYMENT REQUIREMENTS

> Child Support Unit
> P.O. Box 123
> Anywhere ME 12345
> Telephone: (012) 123-4567
> Fax: (999) 444-5555

Account No.: 123456
Payment Ordered $ 100.00 per week
First payment due January 1, 2004

The Family Court has ordered that you make your payments to the Support Collection agency.

This order is payable to the Support Collection Unit through Income Execution (wage deduction) unless the order states otherwise. For petitioners receiving public assistance, payments must be made by Income Execution. Until support is deducted from your wages or income, you must make payments to keep the account up to date.

Payment procedures

Payment can be made by money order or certified check. Mail the payment coupon and include your name, account number and social security number on the payment.

Mail payment to:
Support Collection Unit
P.O. Box 0000
Anywhere, ME 12345

The payment information notice may also include addresses or telephone numbers to contact for information about your account. It is a good idea to transfer this information to your contact sheet or diary. Telephone calls and letters are important communication tools. They enable you to maintain contact with the collection agency. Whether you pay through CSCU or pay the mother directly, it is very important that you keep a log or file record of each support payment made. (A sample payment log is included in Appendix H.)

Payment Log

Docket Number or Case number_____
Child support collection unit account number _____
Children_____
Child support amount _____ per (month) or (week)
Arrears payment _____

Month	owed	paid	balance due
Jan		_____	_____
Feb		_____	_____
Mar		_____	_____
April		_____	_____
May		_____	_____
June		_____	_____

July	_____	_____
Aug	_____	_____
Sep	_____	_____
Oct	_____	_____
Nov	_____	_____
Dec	_____	_____
Year _____	Total amount owed _____	

Other important information to keep at your fingertips includes: the name of the support collection officer, the address and telephone number of the person last contacted, the date contact was made, and the amount of child support arrears (back child support paid and still outstanding). Short notes on each telephone contact should be made during and immediately after the conversation.

As you begin to write, keep in mind that payment activity should include the dates when you received collection letters, when you sent payments, when you made telephone contact, who said what, and who made what promises. It is a good idea to use your calendar and contact sheet in your Court File to prompt further follow-up. If your court order requires you to pay a percentage of unreimbursed medical expenses, make sure you keep copies of all medical bills to prove you paid your share.

If this is done, the account stays current. When payment is not made as ordered, the current account becomes delinquent. That is when you are going to have problems. Even the best paying accounts experience some delinquency. There are many reasons why payments are not made on time. Payments could be lost in the mail, forgotten about or misplaced. There is potential for human error to occur on both sides. But without taking the initiative, nothing can be done to adjust your child support obligation. That is why communication is so important to the child support collection process. Maintaining written and telephone communication with the support collection unit and with Family Court can help you avoid the unnecessary collection measures. (See chapter dealing with CSEA.)

Now, many states have a twenty-four hour telephone voicemail system, so you can follow up to see if your child support payment cleared through the CSCU. It works a lot like the automated telephone bank account. All you have to do is dial and enter the last four digits of your social security number to get information about your account. The voicemail system will tell you when your last payment was posted to your account. Check to see if your state has an automated telephone system. In some states, you may even be able to go online.

Avoiding Support Problems

The best way to avoid support problems is to pay your support when it is due. Don't allow your child support obligation to become overdue. Pay it on time. That's the best policy. Child support is more than just a debt; if you don't pay it, there are serious consequences awaiting you. You could end up in jail. (See chapter on Enforcement).

How long do I have to pay?

A child support obligation ends only when a child reaches the legal age of majority. States differ as to the age of majority. For example, in New York, the age of majority is 21; in some states, it's 18. A child support order may also end if the child is active in the military or a court has declared the child emancipated.

What if I move or she moves to another state?

Under the Uniform Interstate Family Support Act (UIFSA), the state that entered your child support order continues to have the power to modify it even if either of the two parents moves out of the home state.

The right to appeal a decision

After the court makes the order, either party has a right to object to the Support Magistrate's decision. This is also known as an "appeal." The appeal is simply a request for a higher authority to review the decision. The procedures for objecting to the order should be included in the decision. The Support Magistrate and court clerk do this. If the procedures to make an appeal are not included in your child support decision, it is critical that you contact the court or an attorney immediately. There are time limits on when objections must be filed. Don't run the risk of missing the deadline and losing your opportunity to object.

Remember, when you are filing your objections, make sure that you follow the instructions carefully. Failure to follow instructions can be held against you. If you don't understand something, contact a lawyer immediately.

After you file your objections, a judge reviews the objection. The judge may change the order or send it back to the Support Magistrate or leave the order as it is. If either party disagrees with the judge's decision, the case may be appealed to a higher court. In the meantime, you still have to continue paying the amounts ordered by the court until ordered otherwise.

Suppose she is on welfare?

If the mother is receiving public assistance benefits and there are no arrears (back child support), then the first fifty dollars goes directly to the mother. If you pay less than fifty dollars, then the mother does not get anything. This is done merely as an incentive to get mothers to cooperate in providing information about you to enable the agency to collect child support.

Why do I have to pay welfare back?

When a mother applies for public assistance benefits, she must identify you and assign her right to collect child support to the CSEA.

As long as she is receiving public assistance benefits, she gives up her right to receive child support benefits and any arrears until and unless she provides such information about you. In turn, the government collects child support and any arrears from the father as reimbursement.

Let's say a mother has a child support order against the father. He never pays and his child support arrears build up to $5,000. The mother then applies for public assistance and assigns her right to collect her child support arrears to the government CSEA until she stops receiving public assistance benefits. Let's say she stops after four months and the total amount of public assistance benefits paid to her was $3,000. The government now has the right to go after the father for $3,000 for its reimbursement. The agency goes after the father for the full $5,000, takes its $3,000 as reimbursement and pays the difference of $2,000 to the mother.

What if the mother gets off welfare?

Whether or not the mother no longer receives public assistance benefits, the father is still held liable to the government for any past due arrears up to the total amount of public assistance benefits paid. Any amounts that exceed the total welfare benefit go to the mother. In addition, the father is still liable for future child support payments to the mother.

Can I take my child off welfare?

You may be able to take your child off welfare if you earn enough money to support your child directly. However, if the mother has other children with different fathers, this option becomes problematic because the government cannot separate children in the same household; the mother cannot take only one child off public assistance while the others are still on. If this is your situation, you may want to consider filing for custody of your child.

Notes:

Notes:

Notes:

10

Changing the Child Support Order

As the cost of living climbs, the needs of the children increase and parents' incomes change. Over time, child support orders can become outdated, leaving either parent with a child support order that is unfair. To resolve this problem, child support orders can be adjusted to reflect the changes. States can review child support orders for a number of reasons:

1. Cost of Living Adjustment (COLA);
2. Periodic Review;
3. Compare parents' income.

Each year, the U.S. Department of Labor publishes the annual average consumer price index (CPI-U) for consumers in urban areas. The CPI-U measures the average change in prices for things that you buy for day-to-day living expenses, such as food, clothes, shelter, fuel, transportation and medical services. If your child support order is at least two years old, and the percentage changes in the CPI-U annual average since the year that the child support order was first issued, then your child support order may be eligible for a cost of living adjustment.

What is COLA?

COLA stands for Cost of Living Adjustment. Through COLA, your child support amount automatically increases based on the cost of living increase. Orders that are payable through the CSCU are automatically reviewed every three years for a possible change. Either parent can request the review. Both parents are notified about a possible change in the order.

If you or the other parent disagrees with the proposed change, that parent can request a hearing before the Support Magistrate. After the hearing, the Support Magistrate can change the child support order by increasing it, decreasing it, or leaving it as it exists.

What happens if I can't pay?

If your situation changes and you are not able to pay the amount of child support ordered by the court, you and your Ex can agree to change your child support order. Make sure you file the changes with the court, so that the court has it on record. If you fail to do so, you can be ordered to pay the original order. You have a right to ask the court to review your case and to have the child support order lowered. A court can change your order if there has been a "substantial change in your circumstances." In order to do this, however, you must go back to Family Court and file a petition for a downward modification. When you go into the court, ask the court officers to direct you to the petition room.
You will need:

1. Your docket number/Case number;
2. Photo I.D;
3. A copy of the child support order;
4. Proof of change of circumstances.

File for a Downward Modification

A downward modification petition is the mechanism that allows a court to reduce your child support payment. A lot of fathers make the mistake of just calling the CSCU when their circumstances change. Yes, it is important to contact them to keep them updated as to your employment status and address. However, the CSCU cannot change the amount of your child support order. Only a court can do that. So, in order to change your child support order, you will have to go back to Family Court. In this case, you should contact an attorney immediately. It is very important that you do this right way. Don't put it off. You cannot just refuse to pay. If you do nothing, you will run the risk of the CSEA putting administrative remedies into effect. You also run the risk of a violation petition being filed against you (see chapter on Enforcement).

More important, you don't want to waste time. Remember, a court can only modify child support retroactive (dating back) from the date you file your papers and not when you claim your circumstances changed. That means that you still have to pay your child support at the amount originally ordered until the court changes your order. So, the longer you wait, the longer the child support meter begins to run against you. If you don't have all the money to pay the order, then try to pay as much as you can.

Let's take Jay, for example: On May 15th, he was laid off from his job. But he waited until September 15th (four months later) to file his downward modification petition in Family Court. Here, the court can only modify Jay's child support from September 15th, the date he filed it, and not from May 15th, the date he was laid off. Jay is still liable to pay his child support order from May to September as it was initially determined by the court. He waited too long.

What constitutes change of circumstances?

A change in circumstances means circumstances that affect your ability to pay. Bear in mind, just because you file a downward modification petition does not mean that the judge will automatically lower your child support obligation.

In order for the court to reduce your child support order, your change in circumstances must be due to something unexpected and not due to something you did voluntarily.

You may be tempted to quit or change your job to get out of paying child support. Think twice. Judges and Support Magistrates are quick to spot attempts to avoid paying child support. The court can base your child support obligation on what you are capable of earning rather than what you are actually earning.

For example, say you were making $50,000 as an engineer and you quit to take another job making $10,000 as a cashier in a retail store. For the purpose of determining child support, the court can base your child support obligation on what you are capable of earning ($50,000) as your gross income as opposed to the $10,000 you are now actually earning.

Keep in mind that the court will change the terms of the order only if it finds there has been a substantial change of circumstances. That means that you must bring proof of the reason why you want the court to modify your child support order. Without filing and without proof, there is no issue of modification before the court, and the court cannot consider even the slightest possibility of changing the order. You must file your petition for modification, and you must prove or demonstrate that there is a justifiable reason for modifying the original order.

Justifiable reasons for modifying child support

    1. You got laid off from your job;

    2. You got sick or injured and can't work;

    3. Your child's needs and expenses have decreased;

    4. Your Ex has a substantial increase in income;

    5. Your child has become emancipated (legal age of majority);

    6. You have more overnight visitations with the children;

    7. There has been a change in custody, and your children are living with you now.

    8. Some courts may consider the needs of a second family if the resources available to support that family are less than those in the family before the court;

    9. There is a change in the State Child Support   Guidelines;

    10. In New York, if you have a visitation order and your Ex or custodial parent wrongfully withhold visitation/parenting time, you may petition to have payments suspended.

    If you are the party seeking to modify the order, the document that you will need to fill out in order to begin the proceedings is usually referred to as the "Modification Petition."

The Modification Petition

    A Modification Petition is the paper you file explaining the change in your circumstances. You may be able to obtain a copy of the Petition from the clerk's office in Family Court. In the Petition, you must describe the change in circumstance that has occurred since the last order. The amount of detail that is required to be stated in your claim varies from jurisdiction to jurisdiction. Check to see if the Family Court in your area has online forms. With your Modification Petition, it's a good idea to include proof of the change of circumstance, such as a copy of the termination letter if you were fired from your job. But remember, if you've been fired, it must not be your fault. For example, say you got caught smoking marijuana on the job, and they fired you or you were incarcerated. In such cases, you wouldn't be able to use your job termination as a basis for a downward modification because it was your fault you got fired in the first place.

    After the Petition is filed, but before your case may be brought before a judge, the petition and summons must be served on (delivered to) the other party.

Serving a Petition

There are three basic ways for serving a petition. The first is service by the U.S. Mail. Sending the Petition certified, return receipt requested, does this. This method saves time and money without having to serve the other party in person. (Some allow regular mail, not certified). However, the major problem in using this method is that the person you are sending it to, i.e., the other party, may not sign for the certified letter at the post office. By not signing (by not accepting receipt of the letter), the other party has invalidated having been served. When this happens, you must choose another more expensive means of affecting service.

The second is service by a sheriff or deputy. This method is effective because it sends the recipient a message that the matter is serious. Some jurisdictions allow the service to be made at the respondent's place of employment; others do not. Depending on the jurisdiction, some sheriffs or deputies charge a fee in advance. The sheriff often makes two or three attempts to serve the papers on the respondent. If he is unsuccessful, he sends the Petition back with a notice stating that he attempted service.

Third is service by a private process server. Private process servers are similar to sheriffs and deputies. They are often quicker and very flexible. Many private process servers even offer "rush" service within hours. Most private process servers are listed in the telephone directory. You may also want to inquire at the clerk's office in Family Court for a reputable process server in your area.

Keep in mind that different states and counties allow various methods of one or more of these types of service.

The Modification Hearing

The court then holds a hearing and decides whether or not to change the order. Courts are supposed to refuse to modify child support retroactively. This means that even if the court reduces your future child support payments, you will still be liable for the full amount of past-due child support that accrued before you filed the Modification Petition. That is the reason it is so important to file your petition immediately after your situation changes. Failure to file a downward modification at all may be held against you in a subsequent violation proceeding.

Now we are going to have a little quiz: Bob was ordered to pay his Ex $200 per month for child support. He was working with a moving company. Bob lost his job. What should Bob do?

A. Call his boys and grab a forty-ounce and chill for a while.

B. Run to Family Court and file for a downward modification immediately.

What if she says she needs more money?

If there has been a change of circumstances, either party has a right to file a petition to modify the order temporarily of permanently. This means that while you can file for a downward modification, your child's mother may file an upward modification seeking an increase in child support, if, for example, the child is diagnosed with some learning disability and needs special services.

Example: Roger is paying Kim $400.00 per month for child support. The money is taken out of his check every two weeks. Kim calls him and says she needs an additional $400.00 per month. Should Roger give it to her?

No. Kim already has a child support order. It is not up to Kim to decide how much money Roger should pay. If Kim wants an increase in child support, she must take Roger back to court.

The parties may also negotiate an agreement on the issue of modification of child support the same way they would in an initial proceeding.

Automatic Review

If you are paying child support through the Support Collection Unit, and if you or the other parent makes such a request, your order will be automatically reviewed every three years for a possible change.

Notes:

Notes:

11

What if I Don't Pay?

Some Reasons Fathers Don't Pay

    1. I don't have the money;

    2. She won't let me see my children;

    3. I don't like to be "ordered" to do anything;

    4. She trapped me. She never told me she was pregnant;

    5. I didn't want a child. It was her "choice";

    6. It is not my child;

    7. I have no way of knowing exactly what she uses the money for;

    8. She doesn't need the money;

    9. She doesn't go after her other children's fathers for child support. Why me?

What happens if I fall behind in my Child Support payments or if I don't pay?

    The most important thing fathers need to know about a child support order is that it is the first step towards collecting child support. So, if you fail to comply with that order, you can be almost certain that you will have to deal with the legal consequences. This is especially true if you do not make your payments and your child support order is payable through the Child Support Collection Unit (CSCU).

What is the Child Support Enforcement Agency (CSEA)?

    In 1975, the United States Congress created Child Support Enforcement as an amendment to the Social Security Act, also known as the IV-D Program. Under this federally mandated program, states are required to collect a certain percentage of the total child support due each year. If a state doesn't meet certain performance standards, the federal government can penalize it by withholding millions of dollars in welfare funds.

What is the purpose of the CSEA?

Remember: CSEA is in the business of collecting money from you. The purpose of the Child Support Enforcement Agency (CSEA) is to ensure that child support payments are made regularly, and to collect more child support in order to reduce the welfare rolls. This is accomplished by going after delinquent parents. Every state has child support enforcement offices that are actually separate from Family Court. When you think about the CSEA, picture a gigantic collection machine with teeth.

How CSEA works

The CSEA may become involved at any stage of the family court proceeding and whenever a parent requests their services. Not all cases go through CSEA. Parents can agree to be paid directly without the involvement of CSEA. For parents who request their services, the CSEA operates like a third party enforcement machine. Cases are opened when single parents seek help. A single parent may apply for support enforcement services regardless of income. People who receive public assistance automatically receive child support enforcement services. Child Support Enforcement workers may seem like child advocates, but they are more like taxpayer advocates who are there to make sure that parents pay child support, and not other taxpayers.

The IV-D offices also provide various administrative actions to collect and enforce child support obligations that do not require the intervention of the courts. However, in order to collect support, the child support agency must actually locate you. In order to be eligible to receive public assistance in seeking or enforcing child support, the person applying (usually the mother) must cooperate by giving the agency information about you in order to assist them in pursuing you for the purpose of collecting child support.

How they track you down

There are many ways the agency can find you. Now with technology and tougher child support laws, it is easier to locate a parent. The child support enforcement agency uses computers to search a large number of state and federal data banks to track you down.

Through its Locator Services the CSEA can find out public as well as private information about you. It will check your employment records, hospital records, unemployment insurance records, and all government records including but not limited to law enforcement records, social security department records, vital statistics, property records, voter registration records, professional and occupational licenses, and through the Department of Motor Vehicles. CSEA will even check utilities, correctional facilities, cable television companies, banks and Internal Revenue Service records. Locator Services also enable the CSEA to access the U.S. Post Office. One of the most critical pieces of information the agency can obtain is your social security number. Many states now have a program that requires employers to report "new hires" to the Child Support Enforcement Program within a certain number of days of hire.

However, timing is everything. The problem with the system is that most of its information may not be current and up-to-date. If you are the type that frequently changes jobs or addresses, it is hard for the agency to keep up. Like the old saying goes, "you can run but you can't hide." It is simply a matter of time before the CSEA catches up to you. And once it does, its collection practices can be harsh and limitless. As we will learn in Chapter 13, the CSEA can use one or any number of collection actions at the same time to collect child support owed without even going back to court.

How is child support enforced?

If you don't make your child support payments according to your child support order, and the CSEA finds out about it, there are a number of tactics that may be used against you. And there are many different ways the CSEA can collect child support.

The CSEA is not limited to using one method at a time; it can use one collection method or several methods together. Either way, the consequences can be brutal.

The CSEA may collect

1. Current child support obligations;
2. Past due child support arrears;
3. Alimony–spousal maintenance;
4. Medical support;
5. Daycare;
6. Attorney fees and other costs associated with the collection process.

The CSEA collection methods can be divided into four basic groups:

1. Arrears/Income Withholding;
2. Asset Seizure/Liens;
3. Persuasive Techniques;
4. Punitive Acts.

What are Arrears?

Unpaid bills add up over time. Before you know it, your overdue amounts can build up to thousands of dollars. When you fall behind in regularly paying off your creditors (the people you owe), or your accounts, you are said to be in arrears. It works the same with child support payments. The amount of child support overdue is also known as arrears. If your child support order is enforceable through the CSCU, it will keep track of these arrears.

Income Withholding

In most states, once arrears reach a certain amount, the other parent can get a money judgment against you for the full amount of what is still unpaid. Then the CSEA can require that your employer withhold the maximum amounts allowed under the law to pay off these arrears. The CSEA can take up to 65% of your net income. It may seem unfair and it is. But it is legal. This can happen because you are required to pay the current child support obligation plus extra amounts on any past due support. Each account in the Support Collection Unit is monitored by a statewide computer system. If you fall behind in your payments, the system will send a new income execution order to you and your employer with an additional amount to be deducted from your wages to pay off your overdue child support (arrears) as well as your current child support payments.

What they don't tell you about income executions?

If there is an income execution order in place in your case, there are things you must look out for. When you get paid, look carefully at your pay stubs to make sure the child support amounts are correct and that your payments are actually being deducted. You also want to make sure that your payments are actually reaching the CSCU. Don't just assume that because your employer is supposed to take the money out of your check, you are getting credit for it from the CSCU. It is possible that your check can say one thing and that the CSCU records can say another. Employers can mistakenly take out either too much money or too little money from your paycheck. It is also possible that your employer can take out the correct amount of money from your check but fail to send it off to the CSCU in a timely fashion, or not send it off at all. In effect, it is possible that the payments deducted never reach the mother.

In either case, now you have two problems: one, the CSCU will not have a record of your payments and you may suffer harsher enforcement tactics; two, your child's mother will be angry with you. If communication is already a problem between the two of you, you will probably be blamed for the missing payments, and she may use it against you when you want to see your children.

What if my boss didn't take the money out of my check?

Sometimes income executions take time getting processed. If this happens, remember, you are still responsible for those child support payments until the income execution goes through. If your employer does not comply with the income execution order, he can be penalized.

Whatever the reason the amount ordered is not automatically deducted from your paycheck, you are not off the hook; you can still be held legally responsible for making those payments. So stay on top of your money. Follow up with the CSCU to make sure your payments were actually sent by your employer. When the CSCU is uncertain about a payment, it can audit your employer and ask for the check numbers or for a list of payments sent out. So can you. I know it sounds tedious, but keeping track of your actual payments can save you a lot of headaches down the road. Do it.

They say I owe arrears.

If you receive a notice from the CSCU stating that you owe arrears, review it carefully. Make sure the amount of the debt is correct. Child support enforcement agencies have been known to make mistakes. The notice you receive should also contain the procedures for contesting the debt. Most states allow fathers the right to contest the amount of the debt stated in the notice. This is your chance to straighten out any possible errors.

The hearing is very informal. But the burden is on you, and not on the agency, to prove that the amount is incorrect. You won't be able to negotiate the current support obligation; the court in your child support order had already set that amount. However, the CSEA may be more flex-

103

ible in negotiating a reasonable payment plan on the past due amounts (arrears). The best way to deal with this situation is to contact the enforcement agency and try to negotiate a reasonable amount before it starts taking money out of your paycheck.

Ordinarily, the CSEA will collect only if a current child support order is in effect. CSEA will not collect if the children are emancipated unless the father owes money to the state.

What if I have no wages?

If you do not receive wages or a regular salary and you have another form of income, child support payments can be deducted from:

1. Unemployment;
2. Workers compensation;
3. Public and private retirement accounts.

In some states, you could be required to post a bond or other form of security to guarantee that you will make your child support payments.

What if I change jobs?

Under the law, you are required to tell the CSCU if you change jobs or addresses. Also, employers are now required to report all new hires to the state. If there is a "match" in their files, the state will notify your new employer to begin taking your child support payments out of your paycheck.

What if I move out of state?

All states enforce child support payments across state lines under a process known as the Uniform Interstate Family Support Act (UIFSA).

What if I leave the country?

If you do not live in the United States, child support payments can be enforced only if the U.S. has an international agreement with the country in which you are now living.

Intercepting your Tax Refund Checks.

Another popular method of collection is for the CSEA to intercept your tax refund check. This is usually done in non-welfare cases or in cases where the father is self-employed and the amount owed is at least $500.00.

They can take other types of income.

In addition to taking your tax refund, states can also intercept other types of income, like court settlements, lottery winnings, and in relation to any judgment where money is owed you.

Liens and Property Seizures.

Liens can be placed on your bank accounts, on your car or house. In a few states, you could be forced to sell that property to pay off the child support arrears. In some situations, your property can be seized. In some states, driver's licenses and other professional licenses may be suspended.

All Licenses are subject to suspension.

Every state has some type of rule to suspend any issued license, including professional recreational, occupational and driver's licenses. Just in case you thought about moving in order to avoid payments, the following example may make you think again. Let's say you live in New York and your driver's license is suspended. You decide to move to California and apply for a new driver's license. More likely than not, since New York has already suspended your license, California will honor that suspension. The same holds true for any license you have that has, for whatever reason or in any way, been suspended.

How your Driver's License can be suspended

There are three ways a driver's license can be suspended:

1. through Family Court;
2. through the CSEA;
3. or both.

Here is how it works. Once your arrears show up on the statewide child support registry, the CSEA finds out if you hold a state issued license. Then the D.A. or County Attorney notifies the Department of Motor Vehicles (DMV), which, in turn, sends you a notice that a license revocation process has begun. According to federal law, you are supposed to receive a 30-day warning and given a form to complete and send to the DMV, which will then issue a 90-day provisional license. But this is not always the case. The problem is that the notice is usually sent first class mail without confirmation of receipt to your last known address. There are time limits within which you must respond. In some states, it is not a lot of time. So, if you move to another address, chances are that you will never actually receive the notice in time to do anything about it.

Consequently, if you don't make satisfactory payment arrangements with CSCU or contest the allegation of arrears, your license can be revoked. This can happen to an unsuspecting father because the notice of actual suspension is sent by certified mail to your last known address.

Let's say you moved and you never told the CSCU about your new address. In effect, you never got the notices; you continue to drive your car or operate under your license, not knowing that your license has been suspended.

What happens if I get pulled over for something else and then told my driver's license was suspended?

Now you have real trouble. Your ticket is more than just a ticket. More than likely, you will end up having to suffer criminal penalties for driving without a valid license. If it is not the first time you were pulled over, you may end up in jail. If you get pulled over and you are from out of state, you may be extradited (brought) back to your state on a warrant for fleeing your home jurisdiction to avoid paying child support. In addition to going to Criminal Court, you will have to go back to Family Court in order to get your license reinstated.

You can contest the allegations of arrears and license suspension.

If you have reason to believe that your license should not have been suspended, you can challenge the CSCU on the suspension. You can contest on the basis of:

1. Mistaken Identification (it's not you);
2. Financial Exemption;
3. Error in calculation (under four months).

If the CSCU agrees to any of the above, then your license will be reinstated. However, there is a time limit in which to contest. You must do it within a certain number of days. In New York, for example, you have 45 days to challenge the CSCU. Find out what the time limits for contesting are in your state.

You can apply for a restricted license.

If your driver's license has already been suspended, you can apply for a restricted license. A restricted driver's license will allow you to drive to and from work.

Can I get my license back?

In order to get your standard or regular license back, you must contact both the Department of Motor Vehicles, or other licensing authority, and the CSCU. You can work out a payment agreement with the CSCU to have your driver's license fully reinstated.

Can the CSCU change my child support order?

If you fall behind in your payments, the CSCU cannot reduce your support order. Many fathers make the mistake of thinking that if they lose their job or otherwise cannot make their child support payments, all they have to do is call the CSCU and it will help straighten things out. Remember that the CSCU is in the business of collecting money. Therefore, you must apply to the court for a modification or contact an attorney. If you are ordered to make your payments to the CSCU, you must send all payments through the CSEA and not directly to the mother. Otherwise, you will not be given credit for direct payments. Many courts tend to view any direct payments as gifts.

Receiving Reminders

In order to persuade you to make your child support payments regularly, the CSEA will send you delinquency notices, automatic billings, and telephone reminders.

Passport Denial

Under the Personal Responsibility and Work Opportunity Reconciliation Act, the Secretary of State can refuse to issue you a passport if your past due child support is more than $500. Likewise, if you already have a passport, it can be restricted, revoked or limited.

Other Punitive Acts

When all the previously mentioned enforcement methods fail, there are other punitive measures that can be implemented against you as a last resort. These include Contempt of Court proceedings.

As a last resort, a citation for contempt of court will be filed against you, alleging that you have failed to obey the child support order. After that, you will have to appear in court, and the judge or Support Magistrate will hold a hearing. If you are found in contempt of court, you could be sent to jail or placed on probation as a criminal.

What happens at the contempt hearing?

At the hearing, you have the right to be represented by an attorney. If you don't have an attorney, ask the court to appoint you one. In New York, you have the right to have counsel assigned if you are financially eligible for counsel.

During the hearing, the party seeking to enforce the child support order will present evidence of your non-payment through the testimony of the Support Collection Unit supervisor who uses the payment records from the CSCU computer system. The court considers the evidence of your non-payment and ability to pay as "prima facie evidence" of a willful violation. "Prima Facie" evidence is the evidence that stands against you by its obvious self. Now the burden of proof shifts over to you to rebut that prima facie evidence by presenting some credible evidence of your inability to make your child support payments. Credible evidence could include your ability to show that there is a mistake or error in the CSCU records.

That is why you want to have access to those records ahead of time before a violation is filed in order to keep up to date on your payments. If there is a mistake, you want to be able to clarify the error; otherwise that error will pass right under your nose and you will pay for the oversight. On the other hand, it's not really a problem if you know for sure that you did not pay.

Can the Court make me look for a job?

Let's suppose that the reason you cannot pay is that you lost your job. You must be able to explain your lack of employment. Some courts will actually order you to provide a job search to show that you tried to get another job.

Do you remember when we discussed the Modification Petition and talked about problems with voluntarily reducing your income? Well, the same rules apply here. You can't quit your job or otherwise cause your inability to pay your child support.

How do I document a job search?

In order to document a job search, it's a good idea to develop a list of when and where you applied for a job. Keep a chart on whom you contacted and what resulted. Also, get business cards and cut out the want ads you made use of. If these things are done, you should have little difficulty showing that you were trying to find a job. Here is an example of a job search log. (I included a sample form in Appendix I.)

Sample: Job Search

Date	Name of Company	Contact Person	Position	Result
5/1	XYZ Co. 123 Street	Mary Smith	Sales	rejection
5/15	ABC Co. 456 Street	Bob Jones	Sales	interview

Important Note: You should initiate a Modification Petition (see Chapter 10) and document your job search before a violation is filed against you. The violation hearing focuses on your ability to pay your child support, so it's in your best interests to initiate the hearing instead of responding to one.

Paying other debts instead

During the course of your hearing, you may be asked to explain how you are able to manage other debts and not be able to pay your child support. For example, take Tony. During a violation hearing, Tony says, "I can't afford to pay my child support because of my expenses." One "such expense" is his luxury car payment of $700.00 per month.

Now, Tony is sitting in court, dressed in a designer suit, sporting gold jewelry like Mr. "you know who I mean!" The judge turns to Tony and says, "If you have no income, then how do you provide for your lifestyle? Who paid for the clothes, shoes, etc? Who paid for that gold watch? Who paid for that gold bracelet? Who paid for your gold teeth?" You get the picture.

Remember this Income for child support purposes is anything you receive that has a monetary value. That value can be imputed as income. The court considers your means and earnings, education level, previous work experience, etc., with the needs of your child's mother in order to determine your ability to pay. The point here is that Tony's extravagant lifestyle showed he had the ability to pay his child support. Rather than pay his monthly child support, he chose to finance a luxury car instead.

Medical Condition

Now, let's suppose you are injured and cannot work. You can't just show up to court wearing a neck brace. You must show proof of your medical condition. Most courts require you to show more than just a doctor's note or prescriptions. You may have to show actual medical records.

What happens after the violation hearing?

After a hearing is held, if the court finds that you violated the child support order, the court must enter a money judgment for the amount of money that has accrued (your arrears).

Willfulness

If the court finds you in willful violation of child support, you may be placed on probation or sent to jail.

Other Enforcement Tactics

Many States are now using other innovative enforcement tactics to collect overdue child support. Some of these tactics include:

Credit Bureau Reporting

Since child support is money you owe, it is treated like a debt. In this situation, the CSCU acts like a creditor. It can report your delinquency to a credit bureau. You may end up with a negative credit rating. If you are trying to buy a home or car, such a negative credit rating may hurt your chances of getting a loan from a bank.

Sheriff sweeps

Here a sheriff or law enforcement agency goes out into an area and rounds up all delinquent dads and arrests them.

Vehicle Boots

In some jurisdictions, when child support becomes delinquent, the CSCU may have a metal contraption commonly known as a "boot" placed on your automobile so that you cannot move it until you pay your overdue child support amounts.

Sell your season tickets

Season tickets to concerts, sporting events, and other activities have a value when it comes to overdue child support amounts. A court may order that they be sold in order to satisfy overdue child support amounts.

Dead Beat Dad websites

Now with computer technology and the Internet, Deadbeat Dad websites are popping up all over. These websites post a database of photos and information about the fathers who don't pay. This is done to generate publicity and humiliate you at the same time. You are pictured like a criminal in a Most Wanted ad.

There are other enforcement actions the CSCU can take without going back to court:

Administrative Enforcement

No court action is necessary for the CSCU to order the following:

1. Income Execution;
2. Income Tax Offset;
3. Lottery Prize Offset;
4. Driver's License Suspension;
5. Property Execution;
6. Liens;
7. Referral to Tax Department;
8. Credit Bureau Reporting.

Court Enforcement

After taking you to court, the CSCU can take these additional enforcement actions:

1. Enter a money judgment against you and set the amount of arrears;
2. Make an income deduction and take additional amounts to pay off arrears;
3. Require you to post a bond or undertaking;
4. Suspend drivers' licenses, professional or occupational licenses;
5. Suspend recreational licenses;
6. Upon a hearing, the court may hold the father in contempt of court for failing to pay child support or give the father a choice to pay or be sent to jail or be placed on probation;

7. If the mother is receiving welfare, the court can make the father "work off" the child support owed;

8. Pay attorneys' fees;

9. Commit you to participate in a rehabilitative program, such as work preparation or a job skills program or a non-residential alcohol substance abuse program, or an educational program.

A word about taxes:

Are child support payments deductible on my income tax return?

Child support is not taxable to the recipient or deductible by the payer.

What do I do if I am married and file a joint income tax return and the IRS intercepted our tax refund to pay child support?

If you are married to someone who has a child support order and the IRS has intercepted your refund in order to pay the child support, you may be considered an injured spouse and eligible to get back the portion of overpayment. You are considered an injured spouse if all or part of your share of the overpayment shown on your joint return was or is expected to be applied against your spouse's past due child support or spousal support payments. Consult with your accountant or tax preparer to see if you qualify.

Can I automatically claim my children as dependents if I pay child support?

You cannot claim a child as a dependent unless the child resides with you for at least six months out of the year. Only the custodial parent has the right to take the exemption. However, the custodial parent can agree to relinquish the deduction for a given year or future year.

This is especially applicable in situations where the non-custodial parent would be the one who would get back more money. This makes sense, because the parents would collectively have more money to put toward the children. However, this could only work if the parties can agree.

Dealing with the Child Support Enforcement Agency

If you have been keeping up with your child support obligation and you believe that you were subject to an enforcement action that seems inappropriate, don't panic. Mistakes happen. You can make a request that the agency take immediate action to correct the mistake. Maintaining your Court File with accurate records helps resolve problems easily.

Contact the customer service department of the Child Support Collection Unit listed on your contact sheet. Request a breakdown of what you paid and what you owe. The customer service representative will give you a printout and review it with you. Make sure you bring your payment log in your Court File. Then compare the printout with your payment log and note any discrepancies. Always follow up. You may have to go back to court for the judge or Support Magistrate to correct the mistake.

Get your court file

Always make sure you have your Court File handy. Pull out your contact sheet and your telephone log.

By Telephone

You may contact the CSCU by telephone. Generally, caseworkers are so busy managing their caseloads that they are not on hand to answer telephone calls from people asking questions about their case. Most CSEAs use a voice mail system. As you are probably aware, voice mail systems can be very frustrating. When you call CSE, ask for the voice mail directory to make it easier to contact someone who can help you.

Leaving messages

If you call the CSEA and have to leave a message on the voice-mail system, remember to speak slowly and clearly and leave your name, the name of the case, your CSEA case number, the date and time of your call, the reason for your call, and a telephone number you can be reached at during normal business hours. When you state the reason for your call, be specific; don't just say, "I'm calling about the status of my case." Once you leave a message, log it on your telephone log.

Speaking to a caseworker

Before you speak with a caseworker directly, it is a good idea to write down your questions on your telephone log ahead of time so that you can stay on top of your situation. When you get to speak with a case-worker, be patient. Be calm. Don't yell. Don't react. You have your questions in front of you. Use them to guide the conversation. After you have spoken with a caseworker, don't forget to follow up to make sure that the problem has been resolved. Keep a record of your discussions. Always get the name of the person or persons you spoke with in the event you have to speak with a supervisor.

Writing to CSEA

You can also communicate to the CSEA by mail. It may be necessary to request an audit or a breakdown of child support payments. There may be a problem with the income execution order, or you may want to notify CSEA of any address changes or change in employer information to avoid problems in contacting you about your child support order. In these situations, it is appropriate to write a letter. Use your stationery and envelopes in your Court File for all written correspondence.

To avoid delay in processing your complaint, make sure you include the name of the case and docket number and the CSEA case number from your contact sheet in your Court File. Keep your letters short and to the point, preferably to one page. Identify the problem you want resolved. Whatever else you do, don't ramble on about how your child's mother is a lousy so-and-so. Some people make the mistake of complaining about issues that the CSEA has no control over. Don't be one of them.

Meeting CSE Agents in person

It may become necessary to meet with a staff worker. In that case, it is better to make an appointment rather than to just drop in and be made to wait for many hours. However, if you do choose to "walk in," it is a good idea to come in early when the agency first opens. Remember, "The early bird catches the worm." Find out if the CSEA in your area allows walk-ins.

If you make an appointment, ask the staff worker what papers or records you should bring to the appointment, and make sure they are in your Court File along with any documents or any new or additional information that may support your case.

In any event, bring your Court File and pull out your contact sheet and/or journal to take notes. It is a good idea to write down your questions ahead of time so you won't forget anything. Make sure you get the staff member's name and take notes about any discussions. Ask for copies of any documents or printouts pertaining to your account. File them in your Court File.

Remember to keep your cool

Discussing money matters can be very stressful, especially when it involves children from a shattered relationship. When meeting with a staff member, be polite and try your best to remain calm. Don't yell or threaten the staff. They take threats very seriously and will resist cooperating with you.

Complaints

After you have made a good-faith effort to resolve your problem within the agency and you believe that your problem or dispute is not being or was not handled properly, you have a right to complain to a higher authority. A supervisor in charge of the unit or a worker assigned to you may review the case personally to determine if any of the agency's staff handled the situation properly. If the supervisor reviews the case and determines either that the agency was justified or that the case was not handled properly, the supervisor has the authority to rectify the situation. If you still do not get results at these levels, most CSE agencies have a complaint department with a staff member who specifically handles complaints.

In order for a complaint to be resolved, there are two things you should keep in mind:

First, your complaint must specifically state a problem that can be solved. A good complaint spells out the problem and tells the reader exactly what you want done about it.

Second, your complaint must be directed to someone who can do something about it (i.e., a supervisor).

Child Support Enforcement Program Director

The director of the state child support enforcement program in your area is the official in charge of administering over that state's child support enforcement program. This is the person ultimately responsible for what all other CSE agents do or don't do.

Elected Officials

At the state level, there are elected officials (such as legislators, the governor, congressmen, etc). Although they do not have the authority to overturn your decision, they can put pressure on the CSE agency on your behalf. It's always useful for you to know the names and addresses, etc., of your State Assemblymen and State Senators. It's also good to know how to contact your district Congressman. You'd be surprised what a well-placed phone call can do for you.

The Media

The media can be used in the same way as the government complaint process. Most local newspapers, radio and television stations have a section for citizen's complaints. Sending your letter to your local television, radio station or newspaper not only puts the child support agency in a position to respond to the complaint, it also creates publicity, which may lead to an on-air discussion about the problem or to a series of articles about child support enforcement. Many laws and policies are changed as a result of publicity.

On the other hand, government cannot take bad press. Most government agencies have public relations departments whose only function is to deal with the media. When a television station or newspaper forwards a complaint to the government, extra care is taken to resolve the matter.

Also, if you are a client who is being served by yet another agency (educational, social service, etc.), and if that agency provides contact resources for its clients, you may want your counselor to intervene on your behalf. You'd be surprised how one agency responds quicker when another agency is involved. It's called "interagency rivalry," in that one can complain about the other, which is something that they all try to avoid!

Similarly, a single phone call from your attorney to the director's office of the local CSEA may produce more immediate results. A phone call from an attorney implies that an Officer of the Court (your lawyer) is involved and aware of your situation.

Notes:

Notes:

12

Visitation Rights

Fathers and Access

Sometimes, circumstances arise where you may not be able to make the kind of child support payments that the judge orders (see Chapter 10). However, you do want to pick your children up on the weekend or spend some quality time with them, when you can. Like it or not, it doesn't always work out the way you want. You may feel guilty because you don't have the money to do all the things that you may want to do for your children. You may feel that you don't deserve to see them. It could be that you get so sick and tired of trying to see your children and getting no response that you pull away from your children altogether, leaving them to wonder if they have a daddy at all.

Perhaps you are like so many fathers who are afraid to assert your rights because you don't know that you have rights to assert. If this sounds familiar, then you are not alone. Every year, more and more fathers lose contact with their children. It's not always their fault. There is a strong tendency among custodial parents to use the children as weapons, or to punish the non-custodial parent. Sometimes, the mother may have turned the children against you and may be doing everything in her power to get rid of you and make sure you never develop a relationship with your children, leaving you feeling stuck, frustrated and very angry. This can happen at any time in your relationship.

Sometimes this happens at the outset, when she gets pregnant. Other times it happens when you leave and end the relationship, or when you move on and find a new relationship. The good news is that fathers do have rights. As you read on, you will find out how you can go about gaining access to your children.

Remember this: once the father signs an Order of Paternity, legally admitting that the child is his, the father has equal rights over the child as does the mother. Unless there is an agreement of rights between them (visitation, custody, etc.), they both have equal access.

Do I still have to pay if she won't let me see the children?

Your access to your children is not tied to your child support obligation. Remember, child support is not payment to see your children. In fact, child support and visitation/ parenting time are two separate issues that in many courts are heard by two different decision-makers.

Children have a right to know and associate with both parents. Neither parent should ever deny the other parent that right. In some states, the denial of access can result in suspension of child support and reversal of custody. In other states, such as New York, for example, you may petition the Court to have payments suspended. However, arrears (back child support) may not be cancelled, even if she doesn't let you see the children. In this book, I use the words visitation because that is the term that is most familiar, and it is used for legal purposes in the courts. For example, in Michigan, visitation is called parenting time. Fathers are not visitors; they are parents too! I encourage all fathers to use the terms, parenting time or access, especially when in court.

Baby Mama Drama

Baby Mama Drama refers to the games and tricks and ploys some women use to manipulate control or get back at the men who had fathered their children. Some mothers will go to any length to get those fathers out of their lives. They will even use the legal system to do it. It's very simple. She will tell lies to the court in order to get restraining orders to keep you away from her and your children. This type of woman knows that the system is basically on her side. And with a little help from the war council (her girlfriends) and her family members, she can maneuver you right out of her life. It happens so often and so quickly. One minute you think everything is "okie dokie." The next thing you know, she has you arrested and served with a temporary restraining order, a petition for custody and a petition for child support, all at the same time.

These legal papers are three of the most potent weapons an angry Ex has at her disposal, and they are the ones she learns to rely on the most. In one fell swoop, she can get you out, get custody and make you pay child support, while also keeping you away from your children. To adequately defend against this unpromising legal scenario, an unsuspecting father will have to hire an attorney and take off from work to spend numerous hours going back and forth to court. When that happens, if you are like most fathers, you get very frustrated and do not want to deal with the legal system; so you just cave in.

Many fathers are apprehensive; they don't believe that anyone in the court system will look out for their best interests. You can spend a lot of time trying to figure out if this is the right thing for you to do. You don't trust the situation or your court appointed lawyer. So, you hesitate to be upfront or clear, giving out only bits of information to the people who are there trying to help you. On top of that, when you do try to work with them and trust them a little, you make the mistake of wanting to see such immediate results right now that you stop cooperating again.

Unlike you, your Ex is relentless in her efforts and she is prepared. She will make the necessary telephone calls and wade through every voicemail box and still stay on the line until someone finally picks up. She will investigate and follow through on every lead. She will use all the advice and information that she is given, and she won't stop until she gets the result she is looking for. By not coping or by copping out, you are working against yourself, sabotaging any good claim or defense you could possibly have.

File a petition for Visitation Rights

If the other parent won't let you see your child, don't fight with her, and don't give in to baby mama drama. Don't react. The proper way to handle this situation is to petition the court and ask the judge to award you visitation rights. By filling for visitation rights, you initiate, you put your Ex and the drama in check.

Now you are on the offensive and she must play defense. If you have been paying child support and she won't let you see your child, the court is the last place she expects you to take her. She will be stunned because now the shoe is on the other foot. Now, she must respond. This may be just enough to end the drama.

After filing for visitation, courts will almost always award visitation rights, unless there is evidence that such visitation would endanger the child. A judge may order an investigation, a home study and a probation report, or a child welfare agency may send a caseworker to interview all the parties, look at the home and make a report to the court.

You can go into Family Court to the petition room and file a visitation petition. Many family courts enable you to go in and file the papers on your own. However, you will more likely need to hire an attorney to represent you during the hearings in court.

The Visitation hearing

On your first court appearance, the judge will arraign the other party and set another date to come back to court to conference the case. If your child was born out of wedlock, paternity (see Chapter 5) must be established before a court can order visitation. Most visitation cases don't go to trial. Chances are your attorney may be able to settle the case and work out a visitation/parenting time schedule with the other side. Usually, after conferencing the case, the lawyers will submit the visitation plan to the judge who makes it an order of the court.

If the parties cannot agree, then the judge will set the matter for trial. Visitation cases are similar to custody cases. Courts make their decisions on what is in the "best interest of the child." In order to assist the court in making a decision, the judge will order a home study and appoint a lawyer to represent the child. Judges rely heavily on the recommendations of the home study and the child's lawyer.

Before a case is set for trial, the judge may schedule a pretrial conference in order to encourage the parties to settle. If your case cannot settle and gets set for trial, it is best to retain the services of a competent trial attorney to handle the trial. For more on trials, see Chapter 13.

Once you get a visitation order, make sure you ask the clerk of the court for a "certified copy of the order." They know what that means. Also, make sure it spells out the specific frame of circumstances under which visitation is to be undertaken. In other words, make sure it spells out what days, how long, where the visitation exchange will take place, who picks up and who drops off. It is very difficult if not impossible to enforce an order that just simply says "reasonable visitation."

Supervised Temporary Visitation

A judge may also order that visitation be monitored by a third person or agency, where there are allegations of abuse or parental neglect. This is known as supervised visitation. Supervisors may include a grandparent, social worker, law enforcement agent, friend, or relative.

Depending on the circumstances of the case, supervised visitation orders may be temporary or permanent. For instance, a judge may order supervised visitation temporarily while a visitation or custody case is pending or until a parent completes a parenting program or substance abuse program. If there were allegations of abuse or neglect, a judge may order temporary supervised visits pending the outcome of an investigation.

Many fathers get frustrated and don't like the thought of someone watching them with their children like a specimen through a microscope. If this is the case, you must understand that it is more important to stay connected to your children, especially during a custody or visitation case. Children need to have consistent contact with their parents.

It's a hard but necessary sacrifice you must make as a parent. Even if all you do is show up for fifteen minutes, that's more than enough time to give your child a hug and say, "I love you." You must play ball. Do it for your children.

Check if there is a fatherhood visitation center in your area. Many fatherhood groups have centers set up just for this purpose. If applicable, have your lawyer suggest that if the visits must be supervised by an agency, that you be permitted to go to a fatherhood visitation center. These are father-friendly environments usually set up by non-profit organizations to facilitate visitation. The people who monitor your visits are neutral and may be more sensitive and less frightening to your children. One of the benefits of cooperating with the supervised visitation order is that the monitors keep records of the visitation that could be used in court as a record of evidence that can work in your favor at trial. However, be aware that the records can also be used against you at trial, if you fail to cooperate with the visitation monitors, or fail to show up for visits.

Visit Your Child

When you get a visitation order, make sure you visit your child. Although your failure to visit is not seen per se, as a violation, it nonetheless can be used against you in your custody/visitation case. More importantly, it is a psychological letdown to a child. Your child knows that you are going to pick him/her up and is waiting for you. With children, always do what you say you are going to do.

During Visitation Pick-ups and Drop-offs

Don't:

1. Don't argue in front of your child;
2. Don't fight over the child;
3. Don't discuss your court case with or in front of your child;
4. Don't use your child to send messages to the other parent;
5. Don't make disparaging remarks about the other parent to

your child;

6. Don't have your new girlfriend dolled up in the front seat of your car or with you at your Ex's door when you go to pick up your children for a visit. It's inflammatory and none of her business;

7. Don't show off your new car or other new items;

8. Don't be late for visitation. Most orders have a window of 30 minutes before the other party can cancel the visit. Make sure your order specifies the latitude you have.

Do:

1. Do pick a neutral location a police precinct, a church, (a school);

2. Do check to see if there is a supervised visitation exchange program in your area, especially if you have a pending custody and visitation case, and if you have temporary visitation. This is a good idea if there is a lot of anger and hostility between you and the other parent. One parent drops the child off and leaves, and the other parent picks up the child without having to make contact with the other parent. The visitation center is a neutral agency that can document the transfer (you can have a record for court, if necessary, as well as witnesses, and your child can be in an emotionally safe environment);

3. Do take a copy of your court order for visitation/access to show that you are supposed to be with your children on that date and at that time;

4. Do take a tape recorder with you. Set it to record from the time you get to the house or location until you leave. Let the tape roll to show how much time went by. Keep it running as you leave;

5. If there is dissension between you and your Ex, do have a neutral third person go to the door to pick up the children while you stay in the car out of view.

Interference with Visitation

Interference with visitation occurs when one parent without justification physically or emotionally denies or obstructs the other parent's access to the children.

According to a 1994 study by the Children's Rights Council, an estimated 6 million U.S. children have their visitations interfered with by the custodial parent.

Why Does She Do It?

There are countless reasons why this happens; based on my experiences, here are just some of the reasons a parent keeps the other parent away from their children:

To Get Custody

Some parents keep children away from the other parent to gain the advantage in a custody battle. By turning the children against you, she can get them to tell the judge and the caseworkers that they don't want to live with you, so the judge will grant her legal custody.

Control

With some women, it's about control. For this type of mother, the child may be the only thing in her life she can control; so she draws on that as a way to boost up her low self-esteem and feel better about herself. She is using the child as a pawn to make you do what she wants.

Pay Per View Dad

Your Ex may make it so that if you want to see your child, you must pay her money, give her items or do things for her. If she still likes you, she will use the child as an excuse to get you to come over and give her some (attention). She may want monetary favors, even sexual favors. She knows that you love the children and would do anything for them, so she will use them as bargaining chips.

That is not to say that only women are capable of using the children against the other parent. There are many fathers who, upon gaining temporary or permanent custody, tend to do the same thing: use the child as a weapon of control over the other parent.

The New Relationship

In some instances, the mother has moved on and she has found a new man. As her new relationship begins to get serious, she may start cutting off communication with you or start to become hostile toward you just to prove to her new beau that he is the number one man in her life. As the relationship progresses, your Ex may want her new man to be seen as the child's daddy and doesn't want you getting in the way. She may even have her sights on marrying him and creating a family. Her new man probably believes every negative thing your Ex has told him about you; he may see it as your loss because of the breakup of the relationship and now he must fill the gap. You cannot allow that to interfere with the relationship you have with your own children-- no more than you should allow your child's mother to interfere.

A parent may have legitimate concerns

Sometimes the mother may have real concerns about the father's ability to care for the child, particularly when the child is an infant and vice versa. One possible solution would be to have the visit supervised by a grandparent or responsible adult.

Anger

Remember, "Hell has no fury like a woman scorned." If that is in fact the case, then you had better watch out! She is hurt, angry and hostile. More importantly, if she is not able to control her negative feelings about you, she will use the children like a bat against you, especially if you're the one who left the relationship. She could as well feel abandoned. Because of that, she may have determined that you don't deserve to be the children's father, and she wants to strip you of your fatherhood. The failed relationship is seen as a rejection of her, for which she includes the children as a package deal. In such a case, she is not thinking about the children; she is thinking only about herself. Since you don't want to be with her, then you can't be with the children either. She becomes jealous of the love and affection you show your children. There is nothing you can do to change this. She hates you and she wants to hurt you. So she uses your children as the weapon for revenge.

While it is understandable that parties will be angry after a breakup, it is the spillover of such anger and such behavior that interferes with the other parent's access to the children that is the problem. This aberrant behavior is extremely detrimental to you as well as to the children and requires court intervention.

The game player

The father has a visitation order. He calls the mother for visitation and she says no. She has made up some excuse as to why the children can't go. Then on or just after the missed visit, or just before the next court date, she calls and leaves a message telling the father that he can pick up the child. She tells the court, "I tried to allow him the visit, but he never responded," or "he didn't show up."

Now you're in court and it's her word against yours. Unfortunately, this scenario must happen over and over again before most judges will do anything about it. By the time it's resolved, the father will

126

be paying thousands of dollars because this will go on and on for a long time. She is not the least bit intimidated; to her, it's a game. That's how fathers get discouraged; they keep going back and forth to court and they are no closer to getting custody or access. Then they give up; the game player wins and the child suffers.

Filing a Violation of Visitation Petition

If the mother doesn't comply with the Visitation Order, you will need a witness to prove that she did not produce the child as the court instructed her. You may consider asking for a police escort to "keep the peace." Most police officers do not like to get involved in these types of cases. Stay calm and let the officer know that the mother is the one creating the problem. Ask the officer to make a written report if the mother refuses to produce the child.

Next, you will have to go back to court and file a violation petition to hold her in contempt of court. Contempt of court in a visitation case is the same as in a child support case. If the judge finds that the mother willfully violated the visitation order, the judge can impose a fine or sentence her to jail, and, in extreme cases, the court can switch custody. In New York, if a judge determines that the custodial parent is wrongfully interfering with visitation, child support may be suspended. However, arrears may not be canceled.

Don't expect anything to happen right away. Most judges do not like to penalize or put mothers in jail. It may take several violations before the judge loses patience with the mother. Don't get discouraged. Keep documenting each violation. This is where you must use your journal in your Court File to keep notes and dates on missed visits. Your journal will prove invaluable in court. Get a tape recorder, preferably one that works with the telephone. The stories come into court a lot different from the reality.

Are you a victim of parental alienation?

Does the following sound familiar?

1. You call your children, and she refuses to let you speak to them;
2. She makes other plans for the children during your scheduled visits;
3. She cancels your visits;

127

4. You pay your child support order and she still won't let you see your children;

5. You send your children letters and gifts, and she refuses to let the children have them, or she destroys them or sends them back to you;

6. She vilifies you and calls you derogatory names in front of your children;

7. She tells your children not to call you Daddy;

8. She tries to force your children to call her new husband Daddy;

9. She purposely leaves you out of the children's school activities, sports games and other events;

10. She violates your visitation order by refusing to allow you to see your children;

11. Although she doesn't let you see them, she blames you for your children's misbehavior;

12. She refuses to inform you or give you any information about the children's medical, dental, school or other appointments;

13. She has enlisted the help of her friends, family members and others to help her keep the children away from you;

14. She changed your child's last name;

15. She criticizes or refuses to let your children wear clothes you bought for them;

16. She frequently changes her telephone number and address, and forbids her family and friends and the children from giving it to you;

17. She punishes or threatens the child not to give you their address or telephone number;

18. She tells the school officials, clubs, etc., not to talk to you or let you see the children;

19. She is totally insensitive to the child's need to have access to both parents;

20. She punishes the children for talking to you;

21. She sends the children away on vacation and leaves the children with people other than you;

22. She makes important decisions without your input;

23. She refuses you access to the children's medical or school records.

She does any or all of the above while consistently claiming that she wants you to have a relationship with your children and that she is not stopping you from seeing them, but that the children don't want to see you (as if it were their own idea). She further claims that she does not want to force them to see you.

What is Parental Alienation?

If you answered yes to three or more of these scenarios, you are not crazy, but she may be. She could be an alienator and you could be a victim of parental alienation. Parental alienation occurs when a parent engages in physical or emotional interference with the other parent's access to the children. The custodial parent is actually discouraging the child from visiting with the other parent despite a valid visitation order. The scenarios I just described are some of the most difficult for both the child and the parent who is denied access. Unfortunately, there is no effective treatment. Likewise, it is very difficult for courts and professionals who come in contact with this type of situation to deal with it effectively. Usually, the alienator's aberrant behavior is encouraged and often fueled by other family members or spouse. My experience has been that just when the alienator starts making progress in individual therapy, certain family members, such as the grandmother, a sibling or spouse who is not in support of therapy, will actually undo the therapy. Moreover, the legal process does not move very quickly. This gives the mother many opportunities to stall and postpone court dates, enabling her to continue her interference.

As mentioned earlier, judges are not quick to penalize mothers, especially when they have custody of the children. These are just some of the reasons fathers feel a total sense of injustice when involved with an alienator. Incidentally, mothers aren't the only ones who can be alienators. Fathers can be alienators too.

Alienators will engage in the most aberrant behavior to destroy you as well as your relationship with your children. The children are being conditioned to express only the alienator's feelings and point of view, and not their own. I have found that the evidence of brainwashing becomes very obvious when children are asked about seeing their fathers. They will immediately say they don't want to see him, but they cannot actually say why. Nor can they explain their feelings about the situation. Instead, the children will only repeat over and over what the mother had told them.

Alienators are incorrigible. Not even the threat of jail can convince them to stop or consider that what they are doing is wrong. In fact, alienators see their actions as furthering a cause or higher purpose. Anyone who goes against them or stands in their way becomes an instant

129

enemy. It is this persistent core belief that she is right for doing what she does and that there is nothing or no one who can stop her that is the problem.

Alienators will go to any length to enlist anyone who will help further his or her cause. If your Ex is an alienator, her behavior will be obsessive and compulsive.

Alienators will enlist the help of friends, family, clergy, media, and even political figures-- anybody she can convince to share her view.

Alienators become good at orchestrating an entire cast of believers who will even show up in court voluntarily to testify against you on their behalf.

Alienators are angry. The mother may have a deep-seated belief that the father had victimized her. This helps to justify her actions in keeping the children away from him. She believes that she is trying to protect the children from him.

Alienators will even call the other's employer and try to get him fired from his job.

Alienators will engage in excessive litigation to continuously ask the court to punish the other parent by keeping the children away from him.

Alienators become skilled liars. They will use an entire mechanism of lies to keep the drama going and gain every tactical advantage in maintaining custody. They will use false harassment charges and raise false allegations of child neglect and even sexual abuse.

One sure-fire way to tell if your Ex is an alienator is that if she is reading this now, she will become furious.

Notes:

Notes:

13

Going for Custody

Who has custody?

It used to be a presumption that mothers had prima facie rights to custody. This was known as the tender years doctrine. That is to say, preference in relation to custody would be granted to the mother almost automatically, directly because she was always viewed as the primary nurturer of the child. However, since the advent of Women's Rights, in many states, the principle of prima facie rights over the child has undergone changes to the point where little is assumed by the court in relation to custody cases. Both parties are now often presumed to qualify (in the eyes of the law) as primary nurturers. This means that the father is now more often seen as an equally qualifying parent. Although the doctrine of tender years is no longer part of the law, quiet is kept, it still holds sway in the minds of many judges.

Often the custodial parent is the child's mother. Sometimes it is a grandmother or aunt. That person may or may not have legal custody. But because the child is living with her, she has physical custody.

Legal custody gives a parent the right to make decisions about the child's life (where the child goes to school, religious upbringing, medical decisions, etc.). Most of the time, separated parents can agree to custody without going to trial. When parents cannot agree to custody, a Supreme Court judge or a Family Court judge decides legal custody.

Types of Custody

There are four possible types of custody: physical and legal custody, sole and joint custody.

Physical custody refers to where the child will physically live. If the child lives with Dad, then the child's primary residence is with him. It is possible that both parents can share physical custody.

Legal custody refers to which parent can make decisions about the child's religious upbringing, medical issues and education. Just like physical custody, legal custody can be sole or joint. The parent who has sole legal custody is the one who is legally recognized as the ultimate decision-maker over that child.

Sole custody means that the child will live primarily with one parent. That parent is called the custodial parent. The other one is called the non-custodial parent. That parent will be ordered to pay child support and have access to the children in the form of visitation rights.

Joint physical custody means that the parents share physical custody. Here the child spends equal time with both parents. For the child, it is like having two homes. Joint physical custody will only work if the parents live near each other. In some states, such as Maryland, for example, a court may order joint custody, unless there is a reason not to. In New York, there is no presumption of joint custody. The parents must agree to joint custody in New York.

What does a custody battle entail?

Custody battles are fought and settled in court. The cost of litigating custody can be very expensive. Some trials can cost upwards to $50,000 or more. Attorneys get paid by the hour. Some charge anywhere from $200 to $300 per every hour spent in court. From the time the custody action is filed to the time of trial, a custody case can drag on for months. Parties can spend countless hours going back and forth to court, meeting with investigators, counselors, experts, etc., while preparing for trial, not knowing what the outcome will be. This can take its toll on a family, especially the children. In addition, cases do not move very quickly through the court system. Many courts get so backlogged with other cases that it could take more than a year to get to trial. Judges know this. That is why they try to get the parties to settle out of court. If your goal is to get access to your children, it's a good idea to go for full custody and settle on visitation. Either way, you still get access to your children.

Can we settle?

"To win without fighting is best."
--Sun Tzu

Sometimes, parents want to reduce conflict and come to an agreement with one another without going to trial. A peaceful resolution is always in the children's best interest. Trial should always be a last resort.

A parenting agreement puts an end to a custody dispute. The parents sign a written agreement that details their rights and responsibilities, and then submits it to the judge, who signs the agreement, making it an order of the court that can be enforced by any sitting judge.

Custody Agreements/ Parenting Plans

Before making an agreement, do not settle or compromise without knowing all of the facts. You need to discuss the strengths and weaknesses of your case in detail with your attorney and make certain your concerns are addressed before settling your custody case.

A good parenting agreement takes into account the child's need to spend quality time with both parents. When making an agreement, it is a good idea to spell out all of the terms, like who has what and when, so as to avoid any confusion or problems later. Here is where your calendar from your Court File comes in handy. Take your calendar and mark off the dates you will have with your children in red pen. Failure to do so can lead to problems. Also, make sure you get a copy of your child's school calendar. That way you can keep up with school breaks and back to school dates. Having a school calendar makes it easy to plan ahead.

Make sure your agreement includes a schedule for major holidays. It is also important to detail where the pick-up and drop-off location will be. Also, you may want to include a schedule or policy about telephone contact. This will enable you to call your children on the dates and times when they are not with you. This is especially important for holidays when the children are with the other parent.

When making your parenting agreement, be realistic. Don't agree to something just because it sounds good, or because you just want to get it over with. Make sure the agreement will work and coincide with your work schedule and lifestyle. For example: don't set a rigid schedule if you know your work schedule changes from week to week. Never just agree to "liberal" visitation. Before you sign the agreement, take your time and review it to make sure that you didn't leave anything out. Get everything down in writing so it becomes an order that will be enforceable by a judge. Below is an example of some of the things to keep in mind when making a parenting agreement.

135

Parenting Agreement/Parenting Plan

      1. The names of the Children, Date of Birth, Age;

      2. Where the children will reside every day during the year;

      3. What type and how much contact the children will have with each parent [Example: The Child will reside with the mother except for Friday, Saturday, and Sunday from 5PM on Friday to 5PM on Sunday, each week or every other week, or the first week in every month];

      4. Spell out summer vacation, winter vacation, and spring.

      5. For holidays, parents usually alternate between odd and even years. For example: One year Mom has Xmas Eve and Dad has Xmas Day, then the next year Mom has Xmas Day and Dad has Xmas Eve.

Holiday	Dad	Mom
New Year's Day		
Dr. Martin Luther King Jr.		
President's Day		
Memorial Day		
Fourth of July		
Labor Day		
Veteran's Day		
Thanksgiving Day		
Xmas Eve		
Xmas Day		
Easter vacation		
Summer months		
Winter breaks		

      6. Your parenting agreement should also account for special occasions like the parent's birthdays, father's day, mother's day, graduations, etc.;

      7. Your parenting agreement should also provide for who will transport the children to and from their visitation and where pick-up and drop-off locations will be;

      8. Each parent shall notify the other parent if the child becomes ill or injured;

      9. Neither parent shall prevent or interfere with telephone or mail contact between the children.

10. Both parents should agree to refrain from saying anything negative about the other parent in front of the children;

11. One parent is to provide the other parent with access to school records and will sign the necessary forms for school grades, and notify that parent of any school programs and activities concerning the children;

12. Neither parent shall remove the child from the U.S., or the state without prior written agreement of both parents. Unless otherwise restricted by a court order, the agreement should include a provision that both parents will give each other written notice of any change of address and/or telephone number;

13. Your parenting agreement should also provide for a method of resolving disputes and provide for periodic review. Consider including a clause that the parties must go through mediation before going back to court;

14. If one parent breaches the agreement, the other can go back to court to enforce the agreement.

When you get your parenting agreement, post it up in a visible place. It is also a good idea to mark your dates on your calendar in red ink. If the parties cannot reach an agreement on their own, another way to settle a custody matter is to go through Mediation or Trial. In either case, you will need to have a parenting plan. Use the parenting agreement as your guide.

What is mediation?

Mediation (also known as conciliation) is the process that gives parents the opportunity to resolve their differences and work out an agreement that is in the children's best interest. It is a good way for warring parents to put down their weapons, open lines of communication, and give peace a chance.

How does mediation work?

Mediation is simple. The parents sit down together with a mediator. Unlike a court, the setting is private and confidential. Mediators may meet with both parties together or individually. The mediator guides and directs the sessions. The mediator will ask questions to get to the root of the conflict and, at some point, help both parents to stay focused on an agreement that is in the best interest of the children.

Mediators are neutral and do not represent either parent's point of view. They don't judge who is right or who is wrong. Instead, they help the parents discuss the issues that affect the children, such as communication between parents, access to schedules, child and/or spousal support. For parents seeking a divorce, a mediator is helpful in determining how the property will be divided and how best to resolve or agree upon tax issues, etc. The good thing about mediation is that it gives the parties the chance to make their own decisions together regarding the best interest of the children without having to have attorneys or a court intervene and decide or negotiate on their behalf.

In some states, mediation is mandatory. If there is a contested custody dispute, the parties must make an attempt to resolve the dispute before the court makes orders in a trial. However, although many states make mediation mandatory, there is no requirement that the parents actually reach an agreement.

Is mediation for everyone?

Mediation is not for everyone. There are some situations in which mediation would not be appropriate. For example, in such cases as where there has been a history of domestic violence and intimidation or substance abuse, mediation would not work. In some instances, a couple with such a history may have an advocate accompany them during the mediation sessions.

How much does it cost?

Most mediation programs are free of charge. Some private or independent mediators charge a sliding fee scale according to your income and what you can afford to pay.

How do I find a mediator?

To find a mediator, contact the court. Most courts offer mediation. You can also contact your local bar association to see if it has a mediation program.

Do I need an attorney?

While attorneys are not necessary in order to mediate, they can help parents reach an agreement. However, if one parent has an attorney, it is best for the other parent to have one also. It is also a good idea to agree that in order for the attorneys to participate both attorneys must be present.

What if we can't agree?

If the parties are unable to agree, the mediator notifies the court.

Sometimes the parties will agree on some things and not on others, in which case the mediator notifies the court. The remaining issues may continue through the court process.

Can I change my mind about the agreement?

The mediator can cancel the agreement if a party changes his or her mind. The mediator may require that the parent who wishes to cancel the agreement put it in writing.

Who are the mediators?

Some mediators are social workers or attorneys who are trained in dispute resolution. Most states have standards for mediators. Some are actually employed by the court.

What can the mediator do?

Once the parties reach an agreement through the mediation process, the mediator drafts the agreement. Both parents sign the agreement. Then the mediator submits the signed agreement to the court. The signed agreement becomes an order of the court that is legally enforceable.

Mediators can

1. Inform the court when a parent does not show up to mediation;

2. Recommend a child custody evaluation, if the parents cannot agree on custody;

3. Report alleged incidences of child abuse and neglect to Child Protective Services;

4. Report a parent who threatens to harm himself, herself, or others.

Points to consider when talking to a mediator

1. The mediator sets the ground rules and explains how the mediation process will work;

2. The mediator should tell you about his/her training, qualifications and experience;

3. The mediator should demonstrate an awareness of the issues you want to address in mediation;

4. The mediator should tell you up front if there are any fees involved.

Points to consider when going through mediation

1. Mediators must be neutral and not take sides;

2. Mediators must maintain confidentiality. This means that they can not disclose your information without your consent;

3. You should feel comfortable talking to the mediator and feel assured that all the issues are being addressed;

4. When the mediator is present, you should feel better able to communicate and negotiate with the other parent;

5. Any agreement you reach with the other parent is fair and accurately reflects what went on in mediation.

Notes:

Notes:

14

Going to Trial

Custody trials are like war. They are fought on the battleground called the court system. The court system is a reactionary system. It is there to hear a case, make a decision and move on. There are rules that govern the cases and the court. Once you draw your sword by filing for custody, you must be prepared for the battles ahead. You must familiarize yourself with the process so that you won't be intimidated. You can overcome your fear and stand up and fight, but before you do, you must know the art of war.

What happens in a custody and/or visitation battle?

In a custody battle, both parents prepare for war. They hire lawyers to represent them in court. Each side presents his/her case to the judge through evidence and witnesses to show that he/she is right and the other side is wrong. Each side builds up a strong case and cuts holes in the other parent's case by pointing out the weaknesses. The lawyers put on evidence to convince the judge that it is in the best interest of the children for their client to have custody. They also present evidence as to why the other parent should be denied custody.

They do this by trying to convince the judge that all or most of the factors we will discuss later tip in their favor over the other parent. Judges are there to make a decision about who wins and who loses. As in any lawsuit, one of the parties must always lose. In a custody battle, the children are at stake. That's why there are really no winners in Family Court.

Who can file for custody?

Depending on the laws of your state, grandparents, aunts, uncles, or others may file for custody. All states now have laws that give grandparents some type of visitation, so grandparents can file for visitation as well as for custody.

If the parents are not married, paternity must be established before a court can order visitation or custody.

The parties in a custody case

The person who files the petition is called the **petitioner**. The person who files a complaint is called the **plaintiff**. The person who is served the petition is called the **respondent**. The person who is served the complaint is called the **defendant**.

The child is called the **subject child**. The person who represents the child is called the **law guardian** or **guardian ad litem**.

Before you file for custody

Before you go running off to the courthouse, consider the following:

1. Know for sure that you want custody;
2. Know if the children want to live with you;
3. You need a parenting plan;
4. You need an attorney. Do not represent yourself;
5. You must work with your attorney to develop a game plan;
6. Your life will be an open book;
7. Be prepared to spend money on legal fees and time in court.

How do I file a custody case?

Married parents may file a petition or complaint for custody and/or visitation as part of a divorce, separation or annulment. If the parties are not married, they can file the petition or complaint as a separate case. Make sure your petition states custody and/or visitation. That way, you keep your options open. If you later settle on custody, you will still be able to obtain visitation without having to go back into court.

Do I need a lawyer?

No father should walk into a custody proceeding without an attorney. Make no mistake; custody is a very serious legal matter that requires thorough preparation and the skill of a professional. There are many tips in this book that can save you time and legal fees, but there is no alternative to sound professional legal representation. Therefore, if you are going to trial, it is best to consult with an experienced custody trial attorney. Perhaps, after reading the following scenario, you will understand why.

"Being new to all of this, we had made the error of getting (literally) a Broadway lawyer who specialized in representing entertainers and who had no experience in Family Court. His only tactic was to look for ways to adjourn the custody case over and over again. He believed that the other side would eventually disappear or run out of money to pay their lawyer.

Because all the adjournments were at the request of our lawyer, practically at every point, concessions had to be made on behalf of the other side.

Once we did get to the point at which a hearing date was set, our Broadway lawyer admitted that he wasn't prepared to try the case. He argued before the court that he didn't want to represent us any longer because we owed him money from the last adjournment. While we wanted to go ahead with the hearing, he urged us not to push for one at that time. Since he didn't want to represent us and wouldn't go forward with the hearing, we were left with buying yet another adjournment."

Don't ever let this happen to you. If you haven't already done so, read the section on meeting with an attorney in Chapter Four.

How do I find the law?

Even though you may have an attorney, it is still important to understand the law. You can even do a little homework on your own to better understand the legal issues involved in your custody case, and to help prepare your case for trial. Find out where you can access the laws of your state. You can go to the law library in your area. Many courts have law libraries that are open to the public. **Blacks' Law Dictionary** can be a helpful tool to look up difficult legal terms. You can even go online and access legal search engines.

Here are some legal search engines:
1. www.findlaw.com
2. www.usalaw.com
3. www.lawcrawler.com

Where do I file?

Before you file your custody case, there are two things you need to keep in mind. First, that the court must have primary jurisdiction (the power to hear your case). Second, your case must be brought into the proper venue (where the court is physically located).

When the parents live in different states

When the parents live in separate states, it becomes more difficult to file documents. Sometimes more than one court may have jurisdiction in a custody case and parents don't know where to file. The Uniform Child Custody Jurisdiction Act (UCCJA), which applies in all states and the District of Columbia, gives parents direction on where to file a custody case.

Under the UCCJA, for the court to have jurisdiction over a case, one of four conditions must exist:

Home state. This is the state where the child has lived for at least six months or since birth if the child is less than six months old. Jurisdiction is given to the child's home state.

Significant connection. A significant connection between one of the parties and the child to must be demonstrated to the court, and substantial evidence made available to the court establishing that connection.

Emergency condition. The child is in one state and an emergency situation has occurred that places the child under the threat of neglect or abuse or abandonment in that state.

No other state has jurisdiction. None of the other categories apply and it would be in the best interest of the child(ren) to have custody and visitation determined in that state.

If the Respondent lives in another state, then before papers can be served, the Petitioner will need to get the address of the sheriff's department in the county where the respondent lives. Once you have contacted the sheriff's department, find out if there are any fees. Send the copy of the petition that is stamped by the court, along with a check, and ask that the respondent be served.

What do I file?

Once you have the right court, you will file a petition or complaint for custody with the clerk of the court. To make it easy, I will use the term petition. Now most states have sample-pleading forms to use on the Internet. You can download and print these forms. You can also get blank copies of these forms at the clerk's office at the court. You want to make certain you use the same petition form that your court uses. Since each state or court may use different forms, it is not wise to simply copy just any form and use it as a petition for custody. The court clerk may not accept your petition. That is why I did not include a sample petition in the appendix. Don't reinvent the wheel. Go to the court and get the forms that they use.

Serving the summons

In addition to filing the petition, you will also file a summons. A summons notifies a person that s(he) is being sued. The petition tells the parties involved why they are being sued. Both the petition and summonses are served together on the other parent, usually by a sheriff. Don't try to serve the other parent yourself. States have rules on who can serve a petition. In New York, parties to an action cannot serve summonses and petitions on the other party.

When you go to court to file your petition, ask the clerk how the petition must be served. Also, make sure you get the summons form that is used by that court. In some states, a clerk may send you directly to a sheriff's department to serve your petition. In that case, make sure you give the sheriff enough information about the other parent (such as place of employment, work hours, and when the parent is likely to be home).

It's a good idea to check ahead of time if there are any fees and other documents that must be filed. There are usually fees for serving a summons. When you speak with the clerk, find out how much it costs to serve a summons.

Court clerks usually prefer that you bring two copies of the documents so they can stamp the filing date and case number on them. One of the copies you will bring to the sheriff's office to serve on the other party. The other copy you keep for yourself in your Court File.

Once the sheriff serves the summons and petition on the other party, the sheriff will file what is known as an affidavit or return of service with the court. The affidavit of service is proof that the other party has been served. It gives details on how the summons and petition were served. You will need a copy of this document for court as proof of service. The sheriff usually sends you a copy once service is complete. But if the sheriff doesn't send you one, go to the clerk of the court to see if the sheriff filed the proof of service. Ask the clerk for a copy. Make sure you keep a copy for your records in your Court File. That way when you get to court, if the judge asks for it, you will have it.

The custody petition

The following is an example of a petition for custody. In some states this pleading form is called a complaint, in others, a petition. The face of the petition is called the caption. This is where you will find basic information about your case: such as the court; where it is located; the parties; the case number; and, what type of case it is.

147

FAMILY COURT OF THE STATE OF....
COUNTY OF...

_____X

In the matter of a proceeding under Article 6
Of the Family Court Act

Jane Doe,

               Petitioner,   Docket No.: 1234

   Against

                            Petition for Custody/
John Doe,   Visitation

              Respondent.

_____X

Notice that at the top of the document appears the name of the court. Depending on the state, the court can be: Family Court, Supreme Court, or Circuit Court. Here we used the words Family Court. When you file your petition, the court clerk assigns your case a number that usually appears on the right side of the document. This is known as the case number, index number or docket number. This is how courts keep track of your case.

The parties' names are on the front. Here we used the terms petitioner and respondent. This tells the court who is suing whom. The words petition for custody and visitation tells what type of case it is.

Below the caption, the petition will usually give more detailed information about the parties and the case, such as:

1. The names and addresses of both parents;
2. The names of the children and their dates of birth;
3. The relationship of the parties to each other, i.e., if the parties are married, separated or divorced, or if the parties have never been married;
4. A statement that the court has jurisdiction, and a statement that the parties meet the residency requirements of the state and that the children have a significant connection with the state;
5. What you want the court to do, such as to establish paternity, grant visitation rights, custody, etc.

Once the respondent has been served, depending on the jurisdiction, s(he) will have a certain number of days to respond. The number of days to respond is usually found on the face of the summons. Knowing ahead of time how much time the respondent has to answer can help you plan your next move.

Do I have to file a response to a petition for custody or visitation?

If you are the one who has been served with a summons and petition, you must file a response or an answer with the court. The response is a pleading form that looks a lot like the petition. It starts with a caption, and then answers each allegation in the plaintiff's petition.

What happens if I don't respond?

As we learned in the chapters dealing with child support, your failure to properly respond to a petition or complaint can have serious consequences. Remember, once you are served with a summons and petition, you have a certain amount of time set by law to respond. Your failure to answer or file a proper response can lead to the court granting the petitioner the relief sought in the petition, and you will not have the chance to challenge the allegations.

When you file an answer, you are not just limited to reacting or responding; you can create more options--you can initiate. In doing so, you not only respond to the allegations in the petition, you also can make your own request for custody or visitation. Now the court has to hear you too. You cause the ball to come back to your side of the court, and you get to play offense instead of just defense. Get it?

Similarly, if you are the petitioner and you serve the respondent with the summons and petition for custody or visitation, and the respondent does not answer (file a response), then you can make a motion to the court for a default judgment against the respondent. A default occurs when you don't play proper defense. Just like in basketball, if you don't guard the other player, he will have a chance to score. Likewise, if the court determines the respondent is in default, the court can proceed on the requests in your petition. Now you have the chance to score.

Temporary orders for custody and visitation

Once you have filed your custody case, be prepared for the following course of events. From the time the custody petition is filed until the case is actually brought to trial can take months. Usually on the first court appearance, a judge will make an order of temporary custody to one

149

parent and grant visitation to the other parent to maintain the status quo. That means that, if the parents were living in separate house-holds, and the child was living with the mother, a judge is likely to give the mother temporary custody and the father visitation. This is done to preserve the child's need for stability. Most judges are not quick to uproot a child from one household to another, unless there is a good reason. That's why many parents will file for custody before moving to another residence when they know custody will be an issue.

At this stage of the proceeding, there is very little the court knows about you or the other parent. Setting a visitation schedule enables the other parent to maintain access to the child until custody has been decided. Temporary orders are also a test to see which parent will be more likely to cooperate with the judge's order. At the same time, they allow the other parent access. It's another way the judge can tell more about the parent's ability to be a custodial parent. Judges get angry when parties violate their orders; especially while custody case is pending. A parent who consistently refuses to allow visitation or just cancels visits, with or without an explanation, will raise the eyebrow of the judge. When it comes time to rule, this could weigh heavily against that parent.

After the first court appearance, the judge will set a date for the parties to return to court. That gives the parents a chance to retain an attorney and try to settle the case out of court. Depending on how quickly the court calendar moves, a judge will then appoint the children an attorney and may order investigative reports or psychological evaluations. The judge may order a probation report to see if a parent has a criminal history. If there are allegations of drugs or substance abuse, the court can order the parents to take a drug test or go for an evaluation. These issues are very serious. If you have a history of any of the above, you should discuss these with your attorney, so that you can properly address them in the event they come up during your evaluations or at trial. The same holds true for allegations of sexual abuse or physical abuse. Remember, when you are involved in a custody dispute, your life becomes an open book!

Who's who in a custody case?

In custody battles, the **judge** is not there to help you litigate your case. A judge is supposed to be neutral. (S)he listens to both sides of the custody case and renders a decision based upon the best interest of the child. Find out as much information about the judge ahead of time. Judges have their own peculiar brand of philosophy.

Parents have their own **attorneys** who argue on behalf of their client's interest.

A **guardian ad litem** is an attorney who is appointed by the court to advocate on the children's behalf. The attorney sets up appointments with each parent to meet with the child in order to see how the child interacts with both parents. The guardian ad litem can make or break your case. S(h)e takes detailed notes that go into a report to the judge about who should get custody and why. Yes, the guardian ad litem can recommend custody, and, yes, s(h)e assumes a lot about both parties based upon what has been filed in the court papers!

Law guardian or guardian ad litem?

In Family Court, these two designations are used interchangeably. Generally, a law guardian is an attorney who advocates for the child. In some courts, a judge may insist on keeping the distinction between the law guardian and guardian ad litem; the judge may decide not to allow the guardian ad litem to question witnesses or to present evidence at trial. Some states require law guardians to be certified to represent children in court.

The role of the law guardian

Before meeting with the law guardian, it's important to know the process of how everything works before hand. For the most part, the law guardian is really like an arm of the court. S(h)e knows judges and court personnel. More importantly, the judge knows them. After all, the court appoints them. The law guardian's relationship with the court should not be taken lightly. Usually, what the law guardian has to say holds a lot of weight with the judge. In some states, it is almost law.

The law guardian can file documents and put on witnesses and evidence to support his/her position about what is in the best interest of the child. The law guardian can even ask the children with whom do they want to live.

In a custody case, the law guardian will usually contact the parents to set up an appointment to interview the child. In some cases, the law guardian may interview the child several times. Depending on the court and jurisdiction, the law guardian will interview the parents too. In some states, the law guardian will only meet with the child, and a special investigator will be assigned to meet and interview the parents. The law guardian may also interview collateral contacts, such as the child's babysitter, nanny, schoolteacher, or therapist.

The person who is assigned to investigate really tells the whole story in the custody case. The investigator will usually make a home visit to the mother and the father and lay out all the information and details to the court in a report. Then based on that and on the interview with the child by the law guardian (which does not go into the report), the law guardian will make a recommendation to the court as to which parent should get custody.

However, bear in mind that the judge doesn't have to follow the law guardian's recommendation. Nor does the judge necessarily follow what the child says s(he) wishes. This is especially true for a child of very young age. Judges typically pay attention to a child who is at least twelve or thirteen years old. For example, in Georgia, children 14 and over have the controlling right to choose which parent they want to live with, unless the parent has been deemed unfit. But with a five year-old who says, "I want to live with Daddy," a court will not necessarily go along with it. Sometimes, a judge may even interview the child to help determine the child's best interest.

Remember, you must make a complete record in the court on your position. Don't expect anyone else to make your case for you.

Meeting with investigators

Investigators are assigned to gather information about the parents and the child and report to the judge. Before you meet with an investigator, you need to do a little homework. Look at the factors the court uses to determine custody. You want to focus on those and present a clear healthy picture. It's a good idea to meet with your attorney before meeting with investigators and make notes in your journal with questions about your case. You want to make sure the investigator is familiar with the history of the case, and you don't want to forget key points.

If your case involves issues of interference with visitation and/or parental alienation, make sure you alert the investigator. Don't expect that person to just pick up on it. Keep your journal with notes of missed visits, police reports and copies of the order. When meeting with the investigator or guardian ad litem, keep in mind that you will be under scrutiny from the moment you walk through the door.

Investigators are trained to pay attention to details. They look at everything you do and say. They write down what time you arrived, and if you were late. Did you telephone first? (That goes to how responsible you are.) They note their first impression about you. They make notes about you and your appearance. If you appear angry or reluctant to answer questions, they will interpret that as being hostile and uncooperative. Careful, don't react. It is important to cooperate with the investigator.

Meeting with the guardian ad litem

In some instances, a law guardian will not speak directly with a parent who is represented by an attorney. Understand that the advocate for the child is usually an attorney, thus, under the law of ethics, an attorney may not speak directly to a party in the lawsuit when another attorney represents that party. You can, however, get around this by getting permission from your attorney to speak directly with the law guardian. So, if a parent has something to say, and an attorney does not represent him/her that parent can speak with the law guardian directly.

A competent law guardian will familiarize him/herself with the case, while a not-so-competent law guardian will try to wing it. The incompetents or indifferent ones will never meet with the parties or the child; they will just read the paperwork in the file and claim to be familiar with the facts and circumstances in the case. They will then make their recommendation for custody based on that. This is never acceptable. An attorney who never meets or communicates with his client and/or fails to review the file and attempts to represent that person in court is doing the family a disservice, not to mention committing malpractice.

Make sure your lawyer knows this and the judge too. Put it on the record. Make them do their job!

Sometimes parents are really determined not to let the other parent have anything. I remember one case where the following happened: While the custody case was pending, there was an order for supervised visitation. The person who was responsible for supervising the visitation reported to the law guardian that the child was told not to hold the father's hand, not to sit on his lap, not to kiss him hello or good-bye. In fact, she was even told that the father was not the father of that child, but that her stepfather was her father. The law guardian took that up in court. The law guardian argued that this was outrageous; the father was in fact the child's father and should not be told that he isn't. The judge was not pleased and consequently ruled in the father's favor.

At the beginning stage of a custody proceeding, if the children are with the other parent, that parent has a slight advantage over you. Chances are that from the time the case was filed until the law guardian was appointed could take weeks. The other parent has had all that time to work on the children to say they don't want to see you. You probably don't have any contact or access to the child during this time. The child has been separated from you and the other parent is the only influence over the children.

Experienced law guardians can usually pick up on this pretty quickly, though you can't always count on that being the case. If you believe the other parent has brainwashed the child, you may want to state this in your custody petition to alert both the judge and the law guardian. If the law guardian has actually read the custody petition, s(he) will already be clued in to the brainwashing. Don't be discouraged; this is only the beginning. Stay strong. Don't be surprised if the other parent says that the child doesn't want to see you. Make sure you get an appointment to meet the law guardian with your children. Don't take this lightly.

The law guardian will also meet with your child in private. Depending on the child's age and level of maturity, the law guardian will interview the child in private, and without either parent. The child may reveal some very personal stuff. Understand that in a custody battle, your life becomes as open as the pages in this book. The child may even tell the law guardian which parent s(he) wants to live with. Remember, law guardians are not bound by the child's wishes. They can go against a child's expressed wishes, if they believe it is in the child's best interest to live with the other parent.

Mental health professional

Before the case is set for trial, the judge may order a forensic evaluation on the family. In that case, the judge will either appoint a mental health professional or give the attorneys a list of mental health professionals from which to agree on one. The evaluator will interview the family and those who interact with the family, such as teachers, physicians, and relatives. These mental health evaluators usually interview the family in their office; they don't necessarily go to your home. Mental health professionals will submit a written report to the judge recommending which parent should get custody and why. For court purposes, the evaluator will be qualified as an expert witness who will testify at the custody trial.

The mental health professional is usually a psychiatrist or a psychologist. Some states allow a psychiatric social worker to perform the same task.

Selecting a mental health professional

Before agreeing on a particular mental health professional, it is important that you do your homework and review the so-called expert's background and experience. For court purposes, the mental health expert must first be qualified as an expert in the field. That doesn't mean he or she is one. Nor does it mean that s(he) is familiar with the issues in your case. For example, your case may involve issues like interference with visitation or parental alienation. It is possible that the so-called expert may have the credentials, but has never actually worked with children or has no expertise in forming an opinion on custody. Make sure you review the expert's resume or curriculum vitae. You don't want to find out the so-called expert's only professional experience is that he owned a seafood restaurant, when this is the person who will recommend custody to either party.

Points to consider
1. Check to see if the evaluator has testified before in custody matters;

2. Find out how much the fees are;

3. Find out if the evaluator is board certified;

4. Find out his/her views on custody;

5. (Does the evaluator seem to always favor one parent over the other?);

6. See if the evaluator has published articles on a particular issue that might be similar to your case;

7. Contact the American Psychiatric Association to get a copy of its standards for custody evaluations. This will give you an idea of how to prepare for your forensic evaluation. These standards will also be helpful if you decide to hire your own expert to challenge the court appointed expert's custody evaluation. You can go online at www.apa.org.

Hiring your own expert
Sometimes when the court-appointed evaluator renders a forensic report that is not favorable to a particular parent, that parent may seek to hire his or her own expert. Generally, this is not a good idea. The trouble with hiring your own experts is simply this: You hired them. They will say anything they are paid to say. It is highly unlikely that someone you hire will take the witness stand at trial and recommend custody to your adversary. Judges know this. That is why they give little weight for or against recommendations done by privately retained expert witnesses.

Whereas court-appointed experts are neutral. They do not know the parties in the custody case. They don't have a financial interest in testifying for one party over the other. Their fees are usually split between the parties and paid upfront to avoid this type of bias.

Another problem with hiring your own expert is that the expert rarely interviews the other parent, much less the other parent's collateral contacts. Although your expert may qualify as an expert, he or she may not have done a complete custody evaluation of all the parties in the case. Therefore, the expert's recommendation of custody is inadequate. At trial, the judge will not take it seriously but will give it very little weight as evidence at trial. Here is an example:

A mother hired Dr. Jones, a child psychologist. Dr. Jones, highly educated and distinguished, had graduated from a prestigious university. At trial, he attempted to offer a professional opinion in the custody trial that the mother was the best parent to have custody. He even offered into evidence a written report detailing his reasons. When the mother's attorney had finished questioning Dr. Jones, he came across as an expert.

Then it was the father's attorney's turn to question him. When Dr. Jones was asked about the facts of the custody case, he admitted that he never read the custody petition. As it turned out, Dr. Jones never met with the father, nor did he meet with anyone associated with the father. Dr. Jones also admitted that he was completely unaware that shortly before the trial two different judges in that court had found the mother in willful violation of several visitation orders. One judge even sentenced the mother to 90 days in jail. That judge also switched the child's primary residence from the mother to the father. As it turned out, Dr. Jones was also unaware that the mother had filed false allegations of child neglect against the father, which were later proven to be unfounded. After the father's attorney finished questioning him, Dr. Jones ran out of the courtroom so fast that he forgot his coat.

Hiring an expert for a limited purpose

In situations where the court-appointed evaluator has rendered a forensic report that is not favorable, you may want to hire an expert, not for the purpose of recommending custody, but for the limited purpose of challenging the court-appointed expert's forensic evaluation at trial. At trial, your expert should raise enough questions about the evaluation for the judge to consider. If your expert is successful in picking apart the other expert's report, the judge may rule against the recommendation of custody or order a new forensic evaluation.

What else happens at trial?

At the trial, both parties get the chance to testify on the witness stand as to why one should get custody over the other parent. They will give details about their relationship with the child, as well as details about their relationship with one another.

Both sides will also be subject to and have the opportunity to question each other's side in cross-examination. That's where one side gets to aggressively question the facts that the other side presented during direct testimony.

To be successful in a custody case, a party must be well prepared. That is why it is important to keep detailed records in your Court File. This will enable you to answer questions easily and with confidence. Being organized will also help you work better with your attorney to prepare your case. Yes, your attorney. I don't believe that it is wise to represent yourself in a custody case. You should have a lawyer who is familiar with the court, has experience trying custody cases, and is someone with whom you can work, especially to prepare your case for trial.

Before you have to appear in court, make sure you review Chapter Three: Going to Court. This will give you a good idea as to what to expect. Sitting up there on the witness stand in a courtroom can be very frightening. It's one thing to prepare for court in the comfort of a private setting like a lawyer's office, but it's another thing to go into court in front of a judge and other people. You don't have to be intimidated. To make it easier, it's a good idea to take a trip into court ahead of time just to see the process at work in another custody case. That way you can see how lawyers and judges handle such cases. It's also a good way to pick up on the judge's temperament. By the time you appear before the court, s(he) may not seem so strange and intimidating after all.

Your testimony

During a trial, your testimony is called direct examination. During direct examination, your attorney will ask you questions about your relationship with your child. The questions will usually follow a basic narrative format as if you were telling the court a story. Sometimes the judge may ask you questions as well. Your attorney will also seek to admit into evidence certain documents called exhibits.

Your testimony should focus on the factors courts use to determine custody. You want to make sure you include some of these factors (or the factors in your state, since the laws in every state may vary) when presenting your case to the court.

157

You should be able to answer the most detailed questions about your child very easily, like: Who takes care of the child during the day? Who picks the child up from school? Who meets with the teacher? Who takes the child to the doctor? Is the child on any medication? Who prepares the meals? What plans do you have to maintain the child's care, and to maintain a relationship with the other parent, if granted custody? Most importantly, you should be able to tell the court why you want custody, and why it is in the best interest of the child. As a guide to help you better prepare for your testimony, consult with the laws in your state to include the factors that the court considers in awarding custody.

During your direct examination, there may be a lot of interruptions. The opposing attorney may raise objections to some of the questions or answers. Don't be alarmed! It is court procedure. When the attorney objects, just wait until the judge instructs you to answer or not to answer the question.

Also, the judge may ask the attorneys to approach the bench for a side bar discussion that is off the record. Try to be patient and wait for the trial to resume.

Cross-examination

Once you finish testifying on your direct examination with your attorney, you are not done yet. You will be subject to cross-examination. On cross-examination, the opposing attorney will ask you questions, and possibly the guardian ad litem. Cross-examination is a tactic lawyers use to create doubt in the accuracy of a witness' testimony. The lawyer will ask you questions to set you up and catch you in a lie, or point out other inconsistencies in what you said during your direct testimony, or to bring out certain negative facts that may weigh against your case. In short, s(he) will try to break you down. Don't let this scare you! Cross-examination is a skill that even the most experienced lawyer struggles to master. Your best defense to withstand a lawyer's cross-examination is to be well prepared on your testimony and to remain calm. Don't panic because, once the lawyer sees or senses that s(he) is unraveling you, that builds up confidence in the opposition's lawyer. The opposition is now on a roll. If you want to stop it in its tracks, don't let the lawyer cross-examining you throw you off yours.

Unlike direct testimony, in which you explain your answer and give details, cross-examination questions are usually phrased in such a way that permits you to answer only yes or no. It does not allow you to explain an answer. Here, the opposing lawyer wants to pin you down to a response that is favorable to the opposing side's case. Don't let them bully you. If there is a question you don't understand, say so. When answering a question, don't volunteer extra information. No matter what is asked you, don't let it get you upset or angry. Try to stay calm. That is usually part of the game plan. The opposing side wants you to get angry and worked up on the witness stand to show the judge that you are not the best parent to have custody. Don't play into that hand. Don't react to the question. In this instance, cross-examination requires you to respond only.

If your lawyer feels that the cross-examination was damaging, s(he) will ask the judge for redirect examination. Redirect examination gives you the chance to explain your yes or no answer.

Let's say that you didn't pick your son up for visitation last week because the other parent refused to permit the visit. You may be asked on cross-examination: "Isn't it true that you didn't pick your son up for visitation last week?"

You may be tempted to blurt out the reason why you didn't pick up your son, or get mad because you perceive that the lawyer is trying to make it seem like you don't care about your child. However, that was basically a yes or no question. If the answer is yes, then answer yes.

Your explanation may be that you did not visit because the other parent refused to produce the child in violation of your court ordered visitation. Your attorney may then, on redirect examination, ask you to explain the circumstances of the missed visit. That gives you the chance to come back and show the court even further why you should have custody.

Now the other attorney's attempt to throw you off your game has backfired. Keep in mind that everything that is said in court is recorded and becomes part of the court record.

Who should testify?

Rule of thumb: Make sure you know what each witness may say, and that the witness is qualified to say what s(he) is going to say, and knows the facts upon which s(he) will testify. You don't want any surprises at trial. Also, avoid having witnesses testify as to who should get custody. It will damage their credibility, and it is a waste of time. When preparing each witness for trial, it is important to limit the witness's testimony to the facts that support what you are trying to prove. To better prepare your case, it is a good idea to speak with your attorney about who should testify. Write down the names and addresses of people you think will be helpful to your case. Your attorney can subpoena those witnesses. A subpoena is an order to appear in court. Witnesses who fail to show up can be held in contempt of court, fined or jailed.

Also write down questions for your attorney to ask your potential witnesses. Keep your questions short, focusing on one point at a time. Remember, less is more.

The child's physician

Your attorney may want to call the child's medical doctor to testify as to the child's medical condition and needs. Try to limit the testimony to focus on which parent was receptive to the child's medical needs, how each parent attended to the child's needs, which parent took the child to medical appointments. The witness should avoid trying to give any opinion as to who should get custody, as this will only cause your witness to lose credibility with the judge.

Schoolteacher

These witnesses should be able to tell the court how involved you are with your children, what your child's needs are and how receptive you are to those needs. Don't forget to review your child's report cards and attendance records. These items are usually admitted into evidence at trial as business records. You may also subpoena your child's schoolteacher to give testimony at trial. Some teachers are reluctant to get in the middle of a court battle between the parents. Instead of calling teachers into court at trial, it may be better to have the teacher write letters indicating how they know you and outlining your involvement with the child, as this relates to school.

It's a good idea to discuss with your attorney whether or not to call any schoolteacher as a witness.

Questions to consider

1. Whether you have participated in parent/teacher conferences;
2. How long the teacher has taught;
3. How your child's attendance record stands up; If your child is habitually absent, you may want to put the attendance records into evidence at trial;
4. How your child is doing in school. You may want to put the child's school records and report cards into evidence to show how well or how poorly the child is doing in school;
5. The extent to which the other parent has attended school functions;

6. How consistently notices of these conferences (or school functions) have been sent to both parents.

The child's therapist

Other witnesses may include neighbors, babysitters and your child's therapist. A word to the wise: leave the child's therapist out of the trial. Witnesses should be able to testify as to how familiar they are with you and your child. For example: neighbors may testify that they attended a birthday party with the child, whether or not the other parent was present, and how this affected the child.

What do courts consider?

In a custody case, a court makes its decision based on what is in the "best interests of the children." That means that neither parent has an absolute right to custody over the other parent. In order to determine what is in the best interests of the children, the court weighs and balances the totality of the circumstances. There is no one factor.

Courts also look at how the parents have conducted themselves during the course of the custody hearing. They really want to see if the parents are able to put the child's needs before their own. If the court has issued any temporary orders, the judge wants to know if a parent violated that court order. Did the parent allow or encourage visitation while the custody case was pending? Did the parent cooperate with the investigations? Courts are especially concerned with how well the parent who had temporary custody has complied with the visitation schedule. The court considers a number of other factors.

Typically, the sitting judge may consider the following :

Stability

Stability is one of the most important factors courts consider. Judges are not quick to take a child away from school, friends and family. Likewise, children need stable homes with stable parents who don't constantly move around or change jobs. Courts favor the parent who can better provide a stable home for the children. Courts also look at which parent has more time to be there for the child on a consistent basis. Who has the support of the extended family? Are there grandparents, family members, and/or friends who can help provide care for the child? The court also looks at the length of time the present custody arrangement has been in effect, and whether or not that arrangement should be continued.

The child's wishes

In many states, if the child is of sufficient age, courts will consider a child's wishes to live with a particular parent. A lot depends on the age and maturity of the child. An older child's preference may be weighed favorably, while a younger child's preference may not.

The effect of separating siblings

In situations where there is more than one child, courts don't like to split children between parents, especially when the children are close in age. Sometimes, circumstances may warrant separating children. For example, an older teenage child may want to live with the other parent. Courts will weigh the effect changing custody would have on both children.

The home environment

How a child fits into home life with a parent is crucial. Courts are also concerned with the child's living conditions. Is the home filthy? Are there sufficient bedrooms and furniture? Are there other people living in the home? Which parent can physically care for the child, or will the child be primarily cared for by a babysitter?

The primary caretaker

Courts tend to favor the primary caretaker. This is the parent who takes care of the child on a daily basis, the one who prepares the meals, takes the child to school and to other appointments. This is the one who has demonstrated taking care of the children when they are sick; in the case of younger children, the one who feeds, dresses and bathes them has the edge.

The parent's moral fitness

A parent's lifestyle and morality are relevant issues only to the extent that they impact on the child. In the past, a mother living with her new boyfriend (or a father living with his new girlfriend) was seen as a basis to switch custody. Similarly, a gay or lesbian lifestyle has been used as a basis to deny custody or visitation. Now in most states, a court looks at the totality of the circumstances to determine if and to what extent a parent's lifestyle or relationship may impact on the children. If the children are not demonstratably affected by these relationships, courts will not consider them as a factor.

The parent's financial ability

It takes money to raise a child. Courts consider which parent can adequately provide for the child's basic needs. Courts also take into consideration the financial resources available, including child support. Which parent has the greater earning potential? Courts also consider the parent's work patterns. Can the parent hold a steady job? Which parent buys the food, clothes, and pays the living expenses? Who can better provide for the child's education?

A parent's relationship with the children

Judges want to know how the children relate to their parents. When the children have problems, to whom do they go? How does the parent care for the child? Does the parent show affection to the child? Has the parent always been involved in the child's life, or has the parent ever abandoned the child? How does the parent empathize with the child? Can the parent separate his or her needs from the child's needs? How does the parent discipline the child?

A parent's physical and mental health

Problems with physical or mental health can interfere with the children's health and well-being. These are important factors in determining what is in the best interest of the child. Courts will examine both parents' physical and mental health. Courts look at whether a parent smokes, uses drugs or alcohol. Courts also look at whether the parent has a history of physical or mental ailments.

A parent's misconduct

A parent who seeks custody should be aware that courts look into the parent's past to determine the best interest of the child. Courts examine a parent's arrest record, driving record, and child support record. Keep in mind that the failure to pay child support can work against the parent seeking custody. Courts also look into whether the parent has a history of physical abuse or sexual abuse of the child.

A parent's refusal to permit visitation

Children have a right to know and associate with both parents. Parents have a duty to encourage the parent-child relationship. Judges take into consideration the effect an award of custody might have on the child's relationship with the other parent. Will the parent be able to place the child's needs over his/her own to foster a continued relationship with the non-cus-todial parent? In some states, a parent's refusal to permit or encourage access to the other parent may deem the former parent unfit for custody.

Making unfounded accusations of child abuse

Sometimes a parent will make allegations of child abuse or neglect against the other parent to gain advantage in custody cases. Once allegations are made, the state's child protective service gets involved; the case drags on for months until the agency completes its investigation. This can make settlement almost impossible. A parent seeking custody should be aware that courts consider misconduct of any parent as it impacts on the child. This includes falsely accusing the other parent.

Domestic violence

Domestic violence is considered detrimental to children, and courts will generally make an award of sole custody to protect the abused parent from further harm. Where there are allegations of domestic abuse, courts will order psychological evaluations and home studies to determine the affect that domestic violence has on the child's relationship with either or both parents.

Unauthorized relocation of the parent

Where the parents live is important. Sometimes one parent may want to relocate far away from the other parent. Courts may order that the parent be restricted from moving beyond a twenty-five mile radius. A court can set restrictions on how far a custodial parent can move away from the other parent. The court can also order the other parent who moved to pay transportation costs.

The Custody Decision

In a custody trial, a judge rarely rules from the bench. After the lawyers rest their case at trial, the judge usually announces that s(he) reserves decision and will notify the parties and/or their attorneys of the decision in writing. It could take weeks, even months. The judge and his/her law clerk will now review the case, the evidence presented on the record, the testimony, documents, exhibits, etc. The judge will also weigh which witnesses were believable and which ones were not. Once the judge has determined whether the credible evidence in the record clearly supports one of the parents, the judge will issue a written opinion that becomes the final custody order. Depending on the state, the final order may be called the judgment or decree.

Notes:

Notes:

Notes:

15

The Appeal

As we learned with child support, if a parent is unhappy with a decision, s(he) has the right to appeal to a higher court to reverse the decision. In New York, these courts are called appellate courts. In other states, they are called courts of appeal. Such courts have the power to overturn trial court decisions. A higher court can agree to hear the case and may grant a new trial, giving the parent hope for a different outcome. Likewise, the higher court may also deny the appeal and uphold the trial court's decision.

Every state has requirements for appealing decisions. You should consult with your attorney as soon as you receive the custody decision. There are time limits in which to file your notice of appeal.

Keep in mind that you cannot present evidence that was not presented at trial as the basis for your appeal. Even if the trial judge ruled certain testimony as inadmissible, you had to have covered most, if not all, of your contending points at trial. An appeal is not a new trial, but a review of the one that just took place.

The reason you should be as thorough as possible at your custody hearing is because the judge's decision is not as likely to be overturned by the Appellate courts as it is to be upheld. The edge you need to win an appeal is not there. An appeal is likely to be won when you can demonstrate that the judge was somehow in error.

What happens at an appeal?

Unlike the trial court, an appellate court does not hear any testimony. Instead, the attorneys file a written brief consisting of the objections filed, along with copies of the trial transcript and records of the trial court. The attorneys may present oral arguments in support of their legal briefs. The appellate court reads the appellate brief and decides if an error

169

was made. If the appellate court finds that a serious mistake was made, it can overturn the trial court's decision or send the case back for a retrial.

Appellate courts are not quick to change a trial judge's decision, especially in custody cases. The appeal process is costly and takes a long time, sometimes years. During this time, the child's future stability is held in limbo, while facing the possibility of being uprooted from one home a second time. For this reason, appellate courts do not like overturning a trial court's decision, especially if the record supports it. Appellate judges rarely reverse a trial judge's decision unless there has been an abuse of discretion or an error in applying the law. The reason for this is that the trial judge is in the best position to observe the witnesses and the evidence at trial.

Modification of custody

It ain't over!

As some of you may have already learned, Family Court orders are not etched in stone. Circumstances change. Parents move. Schedules change. Perhaps the visitation order is so vague that it causes problems and needs to be spelled out, or the parents have agreed to change custody.

Sometimes after a custody decision has been made, parents take the law into their own hands and unilaterally decide that they are not going to go along with the judge's decision. This is a big mistake. Just like a child support order, a custody order is enforceable. A parent who refuses to cooperate with the order can be held in contempt of court. The parent who continuously violates a custody or visitation order not only risks losing custody or visitation rights, s(he) can end up going to jail.

In order to modify a custody order, a parent will have to go back to the same court that made the custody order and file a motion or petition to change custody.

How soon can I go back into court?

To keep parents from running in and out of court with modification petitions, some states make parents wait a period of time before being permitted to go back into court, while others will entertain a modification depending on the circumstances.

What if the parents moved to different states?

The Uniform Child Custody Jurisdiction Act (UCCJA) applies to original custody orders and modifications. It prevents conflicting custody orders when the parties are from different states. The custody order remains enforceable, no matter where any parent moves. Moving to another state can, however, serve as the basis for modifying the original order. But it must go back to court.

The Parental Kidnapping Prevention Act (PKPA) prohibits states from modifying any custody or visitation order. That means that anything that replaces or comes after a prior custody or visitation order concerning the same child cannot be changed by simply going to another state. You must appear before the original court of jurisdiction.

What do I need to prove?

When filing for a modification of custody, a parent must explain the circumstances that changed since the custody order was made, and that the change of custody is in the best interest of the child. Make sure the motion or petition explains in detail the effects the change in circumstances has on the child. For example:

1. Since the entry of the custody order, the Respondent has exhibited a hostile attitude toward the petitioner and refused to allow the petitioner to exercise his visitation rights, even to the point of concealing the whereabouts of the child in contravention of the visitation order;

2. Such conduct on the part of the Respondent constitutes a material change in circumstances and is contrary to the best interest of the child in developing and maintaining a relationship with the father;

3. Modification of the Order of Custody/Visitation to make the Petitioner the custodial parent is essential to the best interest of the child because of Respondent's hostile attitude toward Petitioner and refusal to allow Petitioner to visit the child, who will be unable to enjoy the benefits of a warm and loving relationship with both parents unless custody is transferred to the Petitioner. Moreover Respondent's repeated violation of Petitioner's court ordered visitation rights indicates that the Respondent is unfit to act as the custodian of the child.

Once the motion or petition is filed, the other parent must be given notice. The court holds a hearing just as though it were making an initial determination of custody. The parents can put on witnesses and evidence to make their case. Remember, the parent who is seeking to change custody has the burden of proving the change of circumstances. Just like in the initial custody case, the court focuses on the best interests of the child and not of the parent. This, however, is easier said than done. In addition to applying the "best interest" standard, judges must also weigh the benefit, if any, of the change of custody against the disruption caused by the change in custody.

Notes:

Notes:

16

After Custody

Don't give up on your children. Stay connected to them. Send cards and letters. Send email. Give your child stamps and postcards to contact you. Give your child a phone card so (s)he can contact you. Send photos, books or magazine subscriptions so the child knows you are thinking about him/her. For teenagers, send video postcards, telling your child how much you love them and miss them. Give your child addresses and telephone numbers of other people who are close to you.

1. If you are not allowed to contact your child, ask a friend or relative to contact the child for you;

2. Don't stop trying to pick up your children for visits;

3. Try to stay connected with everyone who knows your children (schools, friends, doctors, teachers and relatives);

4. Keep a journal. Write down all of the missed visits, including dates and times. Describe in detail what happened;

5. Get an attorney who is familiar with visitation interference and alienation cases;

6. Ask the court to order family therapy;

7. Keep filing violations. Remember, she will keep doing it so long as she believes she can get away with it. The judge will eventually lose patience with her and penalize her. You may establish grounds for a switch of custody. Some courts have held that a parent who engages in this type of behavior is unfit to have custody. In such instances, a change of custody might be quite possible;

8. Don't let her destroy your spirit. Join a fatherhood support group. It's a good way to talk about the situation. You'd be surprised to learn how many other fathers are going through the same thing. Fatherhood groups can provide useful resources like a list or network of expert attorneys

and other information. Remember, there is power in numbers;

9. Don't give up. In some instances, it could take years before you see your children again. Children who are alienated from either or both parents will eventually seek those parents out;

10. You may want to consider going public and becoming active in your community. Write a letter to your local newspaper. An alienator does not like to be exposed. Exposing an alienator may deter or curtail her aberrant behavior;

11. No matter how hurt or angry you get, don't blame your children; it is not their fault. They are caught in the middle. Keep the faith and keep it with them.

Relocation

At some point, a custodial parent will often seek to relocate to another state or foreign country. This can be the non-custodial parent's worst nightmare. There is a national trend toward allowing parents to move. Many states recognize the right to travel, especially when the custodial parent is seeking better employment and lifestyle opportunities. However, some judges will evaluate whether the proposed move will have a detrimental effect on the child's relationship with the other parent. Some states even require the parent to give 30 days notice to the non-custodial parent prior to the move. This gives the non-custodial parent a chance to file any necessary legal action in order to be heard on the issue.

"Children really don't want to hear or believe either one of their parents is a terrible person."
-- Iowan Tribal

Miguel's story

"I was fortunate to have parents who were not mean spirited. My family broke up when I was seven. Since my father refused to allow "another man" to raise "his" children, my mother had no choice but to leave without taking any of their four children with her.

Since at the time, my father worked at night and slept through the day, it became impossible for him to adequately raise his children by himself. After awhile, he decided it was best to send us to live with his mother (from New York to Puerto Rico) until he could figure out the next best

176

step he should take. From then on, our grandmother remained a major influence over us for the rest of her life.

After about a year and a half, Grandma decided that these children needed to be with their natural father, so she packed everyone up and moved from her hometown to live in New York. She lived with us for an additional two years; that is until my father took another wife.

Both my father and paternal grandmother encouraged contact between the children and our natural mother. Consistently, whenever we had holidays from school. (Thanksgiving, Christmas, Easter, and at least two weeks every summer), we would spend them with our mother, who lived in Philadelphia. No courts were involved in any of this. People with rural backgrounds have a stronger tendency to work out their problems themselves, and this was a major point in my family.

In addition, both our parents seldom, if ever, used their influences over us to speak badly about the other. The worse that my mother ever said was that there were things about my father that she just couldn't accept. She'd say this without elaborating on details until we were fully grown.

The worse my father ever said to us about our mother was that when we'd get older, we'd be better able to understand what happened and determine for ourselves which of them was wrong and which of them was right. While that remark was repeated often enough, and while in and of itself, it clearly spoke to which of the two sides he wanted us to favor, there was never a nasty remark coming from either of them about the other.

This experience implanted within me a yardstick to refer to later on. Breakdowns in communication and relationships happen, and when you learn to consider how human (how strong and weak, clear and confused) we all are, it's not really about "whose fault it was" that a child is now growing up without both parents in the same household. Not everyone can latch on to this idea of "nobody's fault" on either side. It's easier to blame "the other." At some point, though, each of us (who come from broken homes) do have to confront the fact that it did happen, and that instead of blaming one or the other parent, we should each look to learn from both their errors and not repeat or perpetuate the weaknesses we witnessed as children."

Fathers Can Change the System

Despite the recent rising statistics of single parent female-headed households and the negative social attitudes toward men about child support, fathers are fighting every day to be more than just a "concept "in their children's lives. Many fathers, just like you, are ready, able and willing to take care of their children, despite the fact that they are no longer in a relationship with the mother.

But in order to change the system, fathers must take the first step and come together. Many fatherhood groups are forming all over the country to address the issue of family and the important roles fathers play. These organizations provide support groups and parenting programs and offer various workshops and seminars through which fathers exchange information. Joining a fatherhood organization is a great way to raise public awareness to change the attitudes of society. At the end of this book, for your convenience, I have listed some fatherhood organizations that may be helpful.

Another way that fathers can change the system is to get involved in the legislative process. Register to vote. Contact your elected officials. You need to know who they are and, more importantly, let them know who you are. Voicing your opinions can have an impact on the laws and policies that govern the family. You can find and write your elected officials by contacting the Alliance for Non-Custodial Parents Rights (ANCPR) at www.ancpr.org.

Notes:

Notes:

17

Conclusion

Fathers, if after reading this book, you walk away with knowledge about responsible fatherhood and a better understanding as to how the legal system works, I hope that you will become emissaries and spread this information around. If there is one thing that I would like for each of you to do, it is to remember and honor the following:

Real Dads:

1. Real dads don't do to the other parent what was done to them;
2. Real dads encourage a parent-child relationship with the other parent by allowing the child to spend quality time with the other parent;
3. Real dads never ever alienate their children from the other parent. Nor do they allow anyone else, i.e., the grandparents, new spouse or other relatives, to do so;
4. Real dads never disparage the other parent to the child, no matter much they may dislike that person;
5. Real dads do more than just send a check. They spend quality time with their children. They are a part of their children's lives;
6. Real dads don't poison the children against the other parent;
7. Real dads are not like Santa Claus or the Easter Bunny, only coming around when they have gifts and want to play. Real dads actually play a parenting role. They nurture their children and take care of their needs like helping with homework and caring for them when they are sick or have a problem;
8. Real dads don't just go for custody as a way of getting out of paying child support;
9. Real dads accept their financial responsibility;

10. Real dads take care of their children's needs;

11. Real dads put their differences with the other parent aside for the benefit of their children;

12. Real dads keep their promises and do what they say they are going to do. That means that when they say they are coming, they actually show up;

13. Real dads encourage the children to communicate with the other parent (telephone, letters, email, etc);

14. Real dads know and understand that children need to be emotionally free to love both parents without fear of repercussions or guilt for doing so;

15. Real dads don't go for custody or visitation then dump the child off on the grandparent, girlfriend or other person to take care of, just so that they can do what they want;

16. Real dads try to find alternatives to the legal system, such as mediation, to resolve disputes;

17. Real dads don't use the child as a weapon or excuse to get back at the other parent;

18. Real dads know and understand that raising a child is a commitment; they don't run from their parental responsibilities or abandon their children;

19. Real dads don't just complain about the law and the system; they try to make a difference. They get involved in the legislative process; they join fatherhood groups.

20. Real Dads Stand Up!

Notes:

Notes:

Appendix A:
Fatherhood Organizations

The Fatherhood Project
Families and Work Institute
212-465-2044
http://www.Fatherhoodproject.org

National Center for Fathering
10200 West 75th Street #267
Shawnee Missouri, KS 66204
913-384-4661
http://www.Fathers.com

The Malik Yoba Fatherhood Project
163 Third Avenue, PMB 153
New York, NY 10003
212-496-1052

ANCPR
Alliance For Non-Custodial Parents Rights
P.O. Box 883
Midvale, UT 84047
http://www.ancpr.org

American Coalition for Fathers & Children
1718 M Street, Suite 187
Washington, DC 20036
1-800-978-3237
http//www.acfc.org

The Center for Successful Fathering, Inc.
13740 Research Blvd. Ste L-2
Austin, TX 78750
1-800-537-0853
www.fathering.org

The Fatherhood Program
111 John Street, Ste. 750
New York, NY 10038
212-791-4927
www.nyyouthatrisk.org

Fathers With Voices
718-913-9534
www.fatherswithvoices.net

Concerned Black Men
7200 North 21st Street
Philadelphia, PA 19138-2102
1-888-395-7816
www.cbmnational.org

Children's Rights Council
6200 Editor's Park Drive Ste. 103
Hyattsville, MD 20782
301-559-3120
crcdc@erols.com

National Father's Network
Kindering Center
16120 NE Eighth Street
Bellevue, WA 98008-3937
425-747-4004
jmay@fathersnetwork.org

National Center for Strategic Non-Profit Development and Community
Leadership
202-822-6725
http://www.npcl.org

National Congress for Fathers and Children
9454 Wilshire Blvd. Suite 907
Beverly Hills, CA 90212
760-758-0268
http://www.ncfc.net

National Center on Fathers and Families
3440 Market Street, Suite, 450
Philadelphia, PA 19104-3325
215-573-5500
www.ncoff.gse.upenn.edu

At-Home Dad
61 Brightwood Avenue
North Andover, MA 01845
508-685-7931
E-mail: Athomedad@aol.com

Boot Camp for New Dads
4605 Barranca Parkway
Suite 101-G
Irvine, CA 92714
714-838-9392
www.newdads.com

Center For Fathers, Families, and Workforce Development
3002 Druid Park Drive
Baltimore, MD 21215
K_1_odom@hotmail.com

Great Dads
P.O. Box 7573
Fairfax Station, VA 22039
703-830-7500
www.greatdads.org

Mad Dads
National Headquarters
3030 Sprague Street
Omaha, NE 6811
402-451-3500
www.maddadsnational.com

National Compadres Network
1600 W. Maple Avenue, Ste. 76
Orange, CA 92868
714-939-6676
www.nimitz.net/compadres

National Practitioners Network For Fathers and Families
1003 K Street, NW, Ste. 565
Washington, DC 20001
202-737-6680
www.npnff.org

National Latino Fatherhood and Family Institute
5252 East Beverly Boulevard
Los Angeles, CA 90022
323-728-7770
bcc@vfnet.com

Father Matters
National Headquarters
P.O. Box 612473
San Jose, CA 951-2473
1-888-648-0718
www.Fathermatters.com

Father Development Project
108 Whitewood Road, Ste. 4
Charlottesville, VA 22901
434-978-1773
www.fatherdevelopment.net

Fathers & Families
20 Park Plaza, Ste. 628
Boston, MA 02116
617-542-9300
www.fathersandfamilies.org

Men and Fathers Resource Center
807 Brazos Street, Ste. 315
Austin, TX 78701-2508
512-472-3237
www.fathersresourcescenter.org

Fathers Resource Center
430 Oak Grove Street
Suite B-3
Minneapolis, MN 55403
612-874-1509
Fax 612-874-0221
www.Resourcesforfathers.org

Full-Time Dads
379 Clifton Avenue
Clifton, NJ 07011-2642
201-772-9444
Fax 201-772-9447

Institute for Responsible Fatherhood
& Family Revitalization
1146 19th Street, N.W.
Suite, 800
Washington, D.C. 20036-3703
Fax 202-293-4288
1-800-7-FATHER
www.responsiblefatherhood.org

National Fatherhood Initiative
One Bank Street, Suite 160
Gaithersburg, MD 20878
301-790-DADS
1-800-790-DADS
Fax 301-948-4325
www.fatherhood.org

Medgar Evers College CUNY
Male Empowerment Center
1150 Carroll Street
Brooklyn, NY 11225
718-270-6051
www.mec.cuny.edu

Real Dads Network
212-875-7725
realdadsnews.com

Notes:

Notes:

Appendix B:
Sample Court Forms

FORM: 1 Summons (Violation of Support Order)

NOTICE: YOUR FAILURE TO APPEAR IN COURT MAY RESULT IN YOUR IMMEDIATE ARREST, IN SUSPENSION OF YOUR DRIVER'S LICENSE, STATE-ISSUED PROFESSIONAL, OCCUPATIONAL AND BUSINESS LICENSES; AND RECREATIONAL AND SPORTING LICENSES AND PERMITS.[1] YOU HAVE THE RIGHT TO BE REPRESENTED BY A LAWYER. IF YOU CANNOT AFFORD A PRIVATE LAWYER, YOU HAVE THE RIGHT TO ASK THE COURT TO ASSIGN A LAWYER. IF AFTER HEARING, THE JUDGE FINDS THAT YOU WILLFULLY FAILED TO OBEY THE ORDER, YOU MAY BE IMPRISONED FOR A TERM NOT TO EXCEED SIX MONTHS FOR CONTEMPT OF COURT.

IN THE NAME OF THE PEOPLE OF THE STATE OF _____ TO THE ABOVE NAMED RESPONDENT:
Who resides or is found at_____

_____

[1] You may qualify to testify by telephone, audio-visual means or other electronic means at a designated tribunal or other location if you reside outside the state or if you are incarcerated and do not expect to be released within a reasonable period of time or if you will suffer undue hardship by appearing in court. A petition having been filed alleging that you have failed to obey the support order dated_____, made by this Court under Article___ a copy of the _____

YOU ARE HEREBY SUMMED TO appear before this Court at (the name and address of the court)_____ (State) on _____, at ____ o'clock in the _____ noon of that day to answer the petition and show cause why you should not be dealt with in accordance with Section 454 of the Family Court Act and Section 5242 of the Civil Practice Law and Rules.

Dated: _____   BY ORDER OF THE COURT

                          _____
                          Clerk of the Court

Notes:

Appendix C:
Child Support Guidelines By State

States that use the Income Shares Model

Alabama	New Jersey
Arizona	New Hampshire
California	New York
Colorado	North Carolina
Connecticut	Ohio
Florida	Oklahoma
Idaho	Oregon
Indiana	Pennsylvania
Iowa	Rhode Island
Kansas	South Carolina
Kentucky	South Dakota
Louisiana	Utah
Maryland	Vermont
Maine	Virginia
Michigan	Washington
Missouri	West Virginia
Nebraska	

States that use the Percent of Income Model

Alaska
Arkansas
District of Columbia
Georgia
Illinois
Minnesota
Mississippi
Nevada
North Dakota
Puerto Rico
Texas
Wisconsin
Wyoming

States that use the Melson Formula

Delaware
Hawaii
Montana

Notes:

Notes:

Appendix D:
Regional Child Support Enforcement Offices
Website: www.acf.dhhs.gov

Region I -Connecticut, Maine Massachusetts, New Hampshire, Rhode Island, Vermont
OCSE Program Manager Administration for Children and Families
John F. Kennedy Federal Building Room 2000
Boston, MA 02203
(617) 565-2478

Region II - New York, New Jersey, Puerto Rico, Virgin Islands
OCSE Program Manager Administration for Children and Families
Federal Building, Room 4048
26 Federal Plaza New York, NY 10278
(212) 264-2890

Region III - Delaware, Maryland, Pennsylvania, Virginia,
West Virginia, District of Columbia
OCSE Program Manager Administration for Children and Families
150 South Independence Mall West, Suite 864   Philadelphia, PA 19104
(215) 861-4000

Region IV - Alabama, Florida, Georgia, Kentucky, Mississippi, North Carolina, South Carolina, Tennessee
OCSE Program Manager Administration for Children and Families
101 Marietta Tower, Suite 821
Atlanta, GA 30323
(404) 331-2180

Region V - Illinois, Indiana, Michigan, Minnesota, Ohio, Wisconsin
OCSE Program Manager Administration for Children and Families
233 Michigan Avenue, Suite 400
Chicago, IL 60601-5519
(312) 353-4863

Region VI - Arkansas, Louisiana, New Mexico, Oklahoma, Texas
OCSE Program Manager Administration for Children and Families
1301 Young Street, Room 945 (ACF-3)
Dallas, TX 75202
(214) 767-3749

Region VII - Iowa, Kansas, Missouri, Nebraska
Administration for Children and Families
601 East 12th Street Federal Building, Suite 276
Kansas City, MO 64106

OCSE Program Manager, Administration for Children and Families
233 Michigan Avenue, Suite 400
Chicago, IL 60601-5519
(312) 353-5926

Region VIII - Colorado, Montana, North Dakota, South Dakota,
Utah, Wyoming
OCSE Program Manager Administration for Children and Families
Federal Office Building
1961 Stout Street, Room 325
Denver, CO 80294-3538
(303) 844-3100

Region IX - Arizona, California, Hawaii, Nevada, Guam
OCSE Program Manager Administration for Children and Families
50 United Nations Plaza, Room 450
San Francisco, CA 94102
(415) 437-8463

Region X - Alaska, Idaho, Oregon, Washington
OCSE Program Manager Administration for Children and Families
2201 Sixth Avenue Mail Stop RX-70
Seattle, WA 98121
(206) 615-2547

Notes:

Appendix E:
Sample Telephone Log

Case number_____

Person Called_____ Telephone number_____

Date_____ Time_____

Contact made   yes   no

Message left   yes   no

Reason for telephone call

_____

_____

_____

_____
Returned call received date_____
Time: _____
Results: _____
Action to be taken

_____

_____

_____

Follow-up on: _____

Notes:

Appendix F:
Statement of Net Worth

Part I A. Preliminary Information:

Employment Status: Self –employed [] Yes [] No
Employer: _____
Address: _____

Hrs. per week: _____ Pay period _____Rate of pay_____
Number of children _____
Names   Ages   Reside with you? _____

_____   _____   _____

_____   _____   _____

_____   _____   _____

_____   _____   _____

Part I B. Income Information:
Gross (weekly) Salary earned last year: $_____
Social Security $_____
Federal Tax $_____
State Tax $_____
Medicare: $_____
FICA $_____
Other Payroll deductions:
_____ $_____
Net Weekly Salary $_____ $_____
Part-time job $_____
Pension $_____
Retirement
Unemployment $_____
        Disability $_____
        Rental income $_____
        Bonuses $_____
        Commissions $_____

Other income:

_____ $_____

Total Weekly Income $_____ $_____

Income declared on last year's

Federal Tax Return $_____

Part II. Assets:

Residence owned [] Yes No [] Address_____

Estimated Market Value $_____

Mortgage owed $_____

Other Real Property Owned: [] Yes [] No

Address_____ Estimated Market Value $_____

Mortgage owed $_____

Savings Account balance $_____

Checking Account balance $_____

Stocks, bonds $_____

Money owed to you $_____

Retirement plans, IRA $_____

Profit sharing, pension, 401K $_____

Automobile   Value $_____

(Year)_____

(Make) _____

Boat, trailer, etc. $_____

_____

_____

Other personal property $_____

Part III. Expenses: [] Monthly   [] Weekly

Rent []   Mortgage [] $_____

Food: Self_____ children_____(school lunch) $_____

Utilities:

         Heat $_____
         Gas $_____
         Electric $_____
         Telephone $_____
         Heating fuel $_____

Water $_____

Garbage removal $_____

Total Utilities: $_____

Clothing: Self_____   Children_____
                                     $_____

Laundry: Self_____   Children_____
                                     $_____

Medical: Self_____   Children_____
                                $_____

Dental: Self_____   Children_____
                                     $_____

Medication: Self_____   Children_____
                                     $_____

Insurance:

Life_____   Auto_____   Fire_____ $_____

Health insurance $_____Accident $_____

Transportation:

Carfare $_____

Toll $_____

Gas/oil $_____

Maintenance $_____

Auto payment: $_____

Balance due

on loan $_____ $_____

Tuition: $_____

Other: $_____ $_____

Total Expenses $_____

Part IV. Liabilities: (Debts, loans, credit cards, etc.)

Owed to_____

Purpose_____

Date incurred_____ Balance due_____
                          Monthly payment $_____

Owed to_____

Purpose_____

Date incurred_____ Balance due_____

                                 Monthly payment $_____

Owed to_____

Purpose_____

Date incurred_____ Balance due_____

                                 Monthly payment $_____

                  Total Monthly Payments $_____

Notes:

Appendix G:
Child Support Payment Log

Docket Number or Case number_____
Child support collection unit account number _____
Children_____
Child support amount _____ per (month) or (week)
Arrears payment _____

Month	owed	paid	balance due
Jan			
Feb			
Mar			
April			
May			
June			
July			
Aug			
Sep			
Oct			
Nov			
Dec			
Year _____		Total amount owed _____	

Notes:

Appendix H:
Sample Job Search

Date	Name of Company	Contacted	Position	Result

Notes:

Appendix I:
Sample Parenting Plan

Parenting Agreement

A. Background Information:

Names of the Children   Date of Birth   Age

_____

_____

B. Residential Matters:

2. Where the children will reside every day during the year.
3. What type and how much contact the children will have with each parent.
__Mother   __Father
From: _____(day and time)
To: _____ (day and time)
Every week   ___every other week   ___other

_____

_____

___During school year other_____

C. Schedule for the summer vacation. The children shall reside with
__mother   __father   on the following days; the children shall
reside with the other parent.

_____

_____

D. Schedule for winter vacation. The children shall reside with
__Mother   __Father on the following days; the children shall reside
with the other parent.

_____

_____

E.   Schedule for spring vacation. The children shall reside with
mother __father   on the following days; the children shall reside with the

other parent.

_____

_____

F. Schedule for Holidays
(Note if Odd/Even/Every Year)

	Dad	Mom
New Year's Dad	_____	_____
Dr. Martin Luther King Jr.	_____	_____
President's Day	_____	_____
Memorial Day	_____	_____
Fourth of July	_____	_____
Labor Day	_____	_____
Veteran's Day	_____	_____
Thanksgiving Day	_____	_____
Xmas Eve	_____	_____
Xmas Day	_____	_____

G. Schedule for special occasions like parent's birthdays, father's day, mother's day, graduations, etc.

Occasion:_____

The children shall reside with   __mother __father   on the following days; the children shall reside with the other parent.

_____

_____

H. No Disparate Remarks:

Both parents should agree to refrain from saying anything negative about the other parent in front of the children.

I. Access to School Information:

_____(parent) is to provide _____(the other parent) with access to school records and will sign the necessary forms for school grades and notify that parent of any school programs and activities concerning the children.

J. Removal for State:

Neither parent shall remove the child from the United States, or the state without prior written agreement of both parents.

K. Resolving Disputes:

All disputes between the parties shall be presented to mediation by_____

The parties must go through mediation before going back to court. If one of the parents breaches the agreement, the other parent can go back to court to enforce the agreement.

Notes:

Index

ORDER FORM
EMAIL ORDERS: Bluepeacockpress.com
FAX ORDERS: 845-348-1964 Send this form.
POSTAL ORDERS: Blue Peacock Press, P.O. Box 1011,
Nyack, New York 10960

Real Dads Stand Up! $19.95

Name_____

Address_____
City_____State_____ZipCode_____
Email address:_____

Charge to: Visa   MasterCard
Money Order or Personal Check

Account Number: _____
Validation Date: _____Expiration Date_____

Signature_____
*New York residents add 7.25% sales tax.
Please add $4 for the first book and $2 for each additional product.
        Total_____

See: http://www.Realdadsstandup.com

Notes:

Notes:

Notes:

Notes:

Notes: